COMPUTER TECHNICIAN CAREER STARTER

by Joan Vaughn

LEARNINGEXPRESS

LearningExpress ◆ New York

Library of Congress Cataloging-in-Publication Data

Vaughn, Joan.
    Computer technician career starter / Joan Vaughn.
       p. cm.
       ISBN 1–57685–096–X
       1. Computer technicians—Vocational guidance.   I. Title.
TK7885.54.V38   1998
621.39'023—dc21   98–10799
                                                       CIP

Printed in the United States of America
9 8 7 6 5 4 3 2 1
First Edition

Regarding the Information in this Book
Every effort has been made to ensure accuracy of directory information up until press time. However, phone numbers and/or addresses are subject to change. Please contact the respective organization for the most recent information.

For Further Information
For information on LearningExpress, other LearningExpress products, or bulk sales, please call or write to us at:
    LearningExpress™
    900 Broadway
    Suite 604
    New York, NY 10003
    212-995-2566

LearningExpress is an affiliated company of Random House, Inc.

ISBN 1-57685-096-X

7 85555 85096 5

CONTENTS

ABOUT THE AUTHOR | Joan Vaughn, M. A., is a technical writer based in Minneapolis, with eleven years of experience in the computer and writing fields. Additional research was provided by Deidre Hayes and Marilou Cook.

INTRODUCTION

WHY ENTER THE COMPUTER FIELD?

Whether you are looking for your first career or are considering a career change, this book is for you! Everywhere you look, you see newspapers and magazines stating that the best jobs now and in the future are in the computer field. There are many ways to break into the computer field, and this book shows you what the hottest computer technician positions are and how to get them, so you can get started in the growing computer field as soon as possible. The high rate of entry-level pay and the rate at which that pay increases make computer careers very inviting. This book will explain what the differences are between the four major categories of computer technicians: software technicians, hardware technicians, network technicians, and Internet technicians.

Most computer technician jobs can be obtained without a four-year college degree, so you can get your career up and running in the shortest possible time. The training required for becoming a computer technician ranges from a two-year associate degree to certificate programs that can be completed within a few weeks or months. The position of a computer technician differs from that of computer programmer, as computer programmers often need to complete a four-year bachelor's degree before they begin their careers. An office manager at a software development company says this about programmers:

> Even though the programmers are in the technical computer field, they don't actually have much expertise installing and using desktop applications. I find that I am the one in the office who installs, upgrades, and maintains our office software.

Many computer technicians are known by other, related job titles. Since this field is relatively new, there isn't a consistent set of job titles throughout the industry. Some alternate job titles that refer to computer technicians are: desktop technician, network support personnel, software trouble-shooter, software engineer, LAN technician, computer service repair personnel, PC system support specialist, and the like. By the time you finish this book, you'll be able to easily recognize all the job titles that apply to computer technicians. This book gives you the information you need to select the computer technician career and training program that are right for you.

In chapter one, you'll get an inside look at what computer technicians do and you'll find specific job descriptions, typical salaries, advancement opportunities, hiring trends, and abilities needed for each job. Then you'll find a step-by-step checklist explaining how you can enter and succeed in this exciting and growing field.

Chapter two tells you why you need formal training and how to select and evaluate training programs near you. You'll find sample courses that are taught in actual training programs for each of the computer technician job titles discussed in this book. These course descriptions can help you decide what occupation is right for you and how long you need to go to school for each one. You can use the checklist in chapter two to ask tough questions to the admissions counselors in training programs you're considering to evaluate the quality of their programs. You'll then discover several tips on how you can make the most out of your training program, such as how to study for exams, taking notes in class, and networking with other students.

In chapter three you can look up the training programs in your area, since the directory of computer training programs gives you a representative listing of schools in order by city and state under each heading. So if you're considering moving to a new city, you can check that city's programs too. All programs provide school name, address, and phone number, so you can contact each school directly to get more information and application forms.

After you've selected a training program that's right for you, you'll find out how you can use financial aid to help you pay for it in chapter four. It clearly explains the financial aid process step by step, so you can be prepared and get your aid as soon as possible.

Once you've completed your training program, chapter five shows you how to land the job you want. You'll find hot tips on where to look for openings and the latest information on networking, writing resumes and cover letters, and using the worldwide web to get your dream job. Samples of resumes from computer technicians are included. Finally, chapter six shows you how to succeed once you've landed your job.

So read on to find out how you can enter and succeed in the exciting and growing computer field.

CHAPTER 1

This chapter explains what a computer technician does and describes the four types of technicians: software technician, hardware technician, network technician, and Internet technician. You'll get an overview of the computer market, the future job market, and salaries available in the computer field. Finally, you'll learn the steps to take to become a computer technician.

THE HOTTEST COMPUTER TECHNICIAN JOBS AND HOW TO GET THEM

Computers are used to perform almost every type of job in every industry, from restaurants to manufacturing to hospitals. People use computers every day to perform important business tasks and share information with others through networks. Since computers are so important in every work environment, computer maintenance and operation are valued by employers and will be still more valued in the future. People with those skills will find themselves in high demand.

Computer service technicians work with every employee in an organization, as well as outside personnel, to provide a stable computing environment. As support personnel, technicians give advice to users by interpreting problems and providing technical support for hardware, software, network systems, and Internet environments. Technicians troubleshoot hardware and software errors, add new equipment, and install, configure, and troubleshoot problems on corporate networks. The job descriptions in this chapter will show you what is involved in these exciting computer careers and how to match up your personal abilities and interests to one of them. You'll also find out what type of advancement opportunities are available for each job. Read on to find the inside information you need to select one of the following hot computer technician jobs.

SOFTWARE TECHNICIAN
Typical Duties

Software technicians act as troubleshooters for desktop operating systems and software applications such as word processors, spreadsheets, and databases. Software companies such as Microsoft® and Adobe® are releasing new products or upgrades to existing products every day, and the people who use those programs require someone on site who understands how they work. The software technician installs

---

Software Technician Job Description
(from a major manufacturer in the Southeast)

1. Responsible for installing and upgrading software applications on both the local area network (LAN) and on stand-alone desktop computers.
2. Responsible for coordinating registration, licensing, and bulk discount programs with software manufacturers.
3. Responsible for maintaining all company software for optimal performance.
4. Responsible for training company personnel or coordinating the outsourcing of this training to ensure the most productive use of company resources.
5. Responsible for troubleshooting software problems.
6. Responsible for the prompt resolution of any software problems to restore productivity within the shortest possible time.
7. Responsible for maintaining contacts with pertinent technical support agencies to ensure prompt assistance when a need arises.
8. Responsible for ordering new software applications as needed to increase individual and company productivity.
9. Responsible for recommending new software applications that will meet the company's needs to perform various tasks efficiently.
10. Responsible for customizing new software applications to best fit the stated needs of the company and to improve the efficiency of the task to be automated.
11. Responsible for identifying the need for new software applications when essential software is not readily available in a prepackaged format.
12. Responsible for assisting departments in the efficient automation of their activities.

---

the software, keeps it running reliably, and may be required to train users or arrange alternate training for them, but the software technician spends the majority of time helping users by answering questions about specific software packages.

Suppose a user is trying to create a spreadsheet of the corporate budget. He works all morning to create the perfect budget and then goes to lunch. When he returns from lunch, he tries to print the file but can't find it; he is faced with having to repeat all that work. What can he do? He calls the software technician. The technician relies on her knowledge of the software and operating system to recover the file and save the user a lot of extra work.

Abilities/Skills Required

Since so much of the software technician's job involves interacting with people and dealing with stressful situations, it is best suited to people with excellent communications skills and a calm demeanor. Though stressful, work in software support offers an immediate reward whenever you can solve a problem or help someone use the software more effectively.

Advancement Opportunities

After you land a job in the computer field, the best way to advance in the area of software technology is to keep current with changes to the software that your company uses. The more you know about that software and how to troubleshoot it, the more marketable you will be. Because it is easier for the technician to support a single manufacturer's software, most companies purchase the majority of their business applications from a single manufacturer. However, if you have the opportunity to attend classes or seminars to learn other software, take it. The table below lists some of the most popular software packages used in industry today.

Word processors	Microsoft Word	Corel WordPerfect	Lotus Word Pro
Electronic mail	Microsoft Exchange/ Outlook	Lotus Notes	Lotus CC:Mail
Office suites	Microsoft Office	Corel WordPerfect Suite	Lotus SmartSuite
Spreadsheets	Microsoft Excel	Quattro Pro	Lotus 1-2-3
Databases	Microsoft Access	Adobe Filemaker Pro	dbase IV
Operating systems	MS DOS	Microsoft Windows	IBM OS2

HARDWARE TECHNICIAN
Typical Duties

While software technicians troubleshoot operating systems and software applications, hardware technicians spend their time repairing, supporting, and maintaining computers and computer-related equipment such as printers, scanners, and hard and floppy disk drives. As software programs become more and more powerful, computers must continually be upgraded to keep pace with those changes, and hardware technicians are responsible for making these changes.

Hardware technicians perform an initial system setup and check diagnostics to determine upgrade needs; install and adjust disk drives; test and install chips, circuit boards, modems, and interface cards; perform minor adjustments and repairs to monitors and printers; repair and replace cables; and perform preventive maintenance.

Computer Hardware Technician Job Description
(from a major manufacturer in the Southeast)

1. Responsible for installing and upgrading all company computer equipment and peripherals.

2. Responsible for coordinating registration, licensing, warranties, and bulk discount programs with hardware and peripheral manufacturers.

3. Responsible for maintaining all company computer equipment for optimal performance, including but not limited to dumb terminals, stand-alone units, industrial and mainframe equipment, and peripherals.

4. Responsible for training company personnel in the proper use of the equipment assigned to them.

5. Responsible for troubleshooting hardware problems.

6. Responsible for the prompt resolution of any hardware problems to restore productivity within the shortest possible time.

7. Responsible for maintaining contacts with pertinent technical support agencies to ensure prompt assistance when a need arises.

8. Responsible for working with engineers to recommend hardware to meet specific industrial company needs.

9. Responsible for ordering new hardware as needed to increase individual and company productivity.

10. Responsible for assisting departments in the efficient automation of their activities.

11. Responsible for coordinating resources to improve efficiency and productivity.

Abilities/Skills Required

This type of job is best suited to people who enjoy puttering with electronics and solving problems. You need to listen to a user's problem, process the information, and propose solutions. These technicians function in much the same way as auto mechanics. If a car owner tells the mechanic his car is stalling, the mechanic takes that information, recalls problems for which stalling might be a symptom, identifies the appropriate problem, and fixes it. Hardware technicians use the same analytical decision-making skills to identify solutions to computer problems.

Advancement Opportunities

Most hardware technicians begin their career as specialists in a particular type of equipment (PCs, UNIX boxes, or Apples). Advancement in this career usually means a promotion to a supervisor or analyst responsible for making decisions about the right equipment and servicing options for a company.

NETWORK TECHNICIAN
Typical Duties

A network is a collection of computers linked together so they can share information or peripherals such as printers. A network of computers within a single office or building is called a LAN (local area network); a WAN (wide area network) connects computers between buildings, cities, even countries. The technology that connects these computers requires constant vigilance and upkeep. The network technician's chief function is to ensure that the network is always available. This requires identifying problems that occur on a network as well as installing and testing network cards, running cables, and training others to use the network properly.

Abilities/Skills Required

Individuals who enjoy problem-solving and methodical work may be well suited to a career as a network technician. Networks rely on the interaction of many small parts (cables, network cards, modems, and software), any one of which may experience problems that result in a loss of the information-sharing portion of the network, or as is commonly heard around the office, causes the network to go down. Detail-oriented individuals will enjoy the challenge of the hunt to find the one part that is causing the problem.

Network Technician Job Description

(from a major manufacturer in the Southeast)

1. Responsible for installing and upgrading hardware equipment and software applications required for efficient use of company local area network.

2. Responsible for coordinating registration, licensing, and bulk discount programs with hardware and peripheral manufacturers.

3. Responsible for maintaining all network computer equipment for optimal performance.

4. Responsible for monitoring the network needs and requisitioning upgrades and expansions as they become necessary.

5. Responsible for training company personnel in the proper use of the local area network.

6. Responsible for troubleshooting network problems.

7. Responsible for the prompt resolution of any problems to restore productivity within the shortest possible time.

8. Responsible for maintaining contacts with pertinent technical support agencies to ensure prompt assistance.

9. Responsible for coordinating needs of all departments and implementing those within the company network.

10. Responsible for maintaining effective security controls within the network.

11. Responsible for maintaining and programming the telephone trunking system.

12. Responsible for maintaining or coordinating the maintenance of company voice mail.

13. Responsible for maintaining or coordinating the maintenance of company electronic mail.

14. Responsible for ordering new equipment or software as needed to increase individual and company productivity.

15. Responsible for assisting departments in the efficient automation of their activities.

Advancement Opportunities

Since every company's network is slightly different from everyone else's, network specialists usually begin each new job as technicians. As they learn more about their company's network and the associated equipment, they can advance to analyst or supervisor. These advanced positions require specialists to educate themselves continually about the changing industry standards.

INTERNET TECHNICIAN

Typical Duties

The Internet is quickly making its move into mainstream businesses, and that has created a need for technicians to ease the way. Internet technicians perform many of the same job duties as hardware, software, and network technicians but concentrate on the technology specific to the Internet, including site administration and server maintenance. They also ensure that the site is as secure as possible from potential hackers.

Abilities/Skills Required

Because of the newness of the job description, those aspiring to a career in this field need to be flexible. The industry is changing so rapidly that the market sees new software and hardware every day. Technicians must enjoy researching, learning, and designing. When asked to make recommendations for future expansions, they need to be familiar with current trends as well as likely future developments to avoid suggesting technology that will be out of date before projects are completed.

Internet Technician Job Description
(from a major manufacturer in the Southeast)

1. Responsible for upgrading the company Internet and intranet technologies to make the best use of available tools and to present the company in such a way as to meet stated company goals.

2. Responsible for maintaining software required to operate the Web sites.

3. Responsible for troubleshooting Web problems.

4. Responsible for the prompt resolution of problems to restore productivity within the shortest possible time.

5. Responsible for recommending equipment and software to meet the specific coordinated needs of the company.

6. Responsible for ordering resources as needed to increase the productivity of the Internet and intranet sites.

7. Responsible for assisting departments in the efficient implementation of their activities and needs as they pertain to the Internet/intranet.

8. Responsible for coordinating resources to improve efficiency and productivity.

Advancement Opportunities

As the Internet's technology becomes more diverse and companies become more comfortable with their role on the Internet, the technician's job will become more specific. Just as traditional computer technicians focus on software, hardware, or networking, so too will the Internet technician's job become divided into those categories. No longer will technicians need a broad knowledge of every subject; soon they will need to become expert at a particular subject: the design, software support, hardware support, or network interaction.

WHY BECOME A COMPUTER TECHNICIAN?
Exploding Job Growth

The computer services industry has grown rapidly over the past two decades, and this growth has created a need for highly skilled technicians. Many specializations have developed, but as yet there are no uniform job titles. Even with this uncertainty, the Bureau of Labor Statistics shows that the industry will continue to grow rapidly in the future, with employment expected to nearly double by 2005. In fact, computer-related careers are among the top five fastest growing professions in the coming decade, and the demand for computer technicians will grow faster than average, with a growth rate of approximately 60 percent.

The demand for technicians will rise because organizations will continue to develop more sophisticated uses for computers and computer systems and more non-technical employees will need to use computers more frequently. As the technology advances, computer technicians will need to upgrade their skills and technical expertise and their ability to interact with users.

Computer technicians will need to be flexible to stay competitive in the job market. Experts suggest that the successful employees of the future will be those dedicated to continuous improvement just to keep up with the changes in the industry's future.

Good Salary

A number of factors affect salaries in any industry. They include supply and demand, employer size, corporate industry, and geographic location.

> **Wanted:**
> **Computer Technician**
>
> Two to three years of experience in PC installations, troubleshooting, and break/fix hardware and software. A+ certification a requirement. Other manufacturers certification a plus. Growth opportunities unlimited. Wages commensurate with experience and certification.

Industry experts acknowledge that salaries for entry-level positions in the computer industry vary greatly, but they tend to fall within the $18,000 to $26,000 range.

Computer professionals increase their salary by obtaining more training and advancing within their chosen specialty. The table below presents information taken from several recent salary surveys and shows the effect the industry's dramatic growth has had on the salaries of its professionals. Keep in mind that you can achieve salaries higher than those listed below by continuously acquiring more training, certification, and experience.

Specialization	1994 average	1997 entry-level	1997 average	1997 high
Software Technician	$18,000	$19,000	$26,000	$40,000
Hardware Technician	$18,000	$19,000	$28,000	$43,000
Internet Technician	No info	$22,000	$34,000	$50,000
Network Technician	$18,000	$20,000	$32,000	$46,000

Minimum Level of Training

You can become a computer technician without a four-year college degree, so these jobs are very enticing to people who want to get through training quickly and land a good-paying job in the shortest time. A human resources manager from North Carolina says this about the training to become a computer technician, based on ten years of experience in the field:

> Some companies state a bachelor's degree is a standard requirement for computer technician work. However, this is not a necessity. You can ask a company to look at comparable skills and experience as a means of waiving the educational requirement. Almost every company will require a GED as a minimum educational requirement. This high school equivalency shows the employer that you have the potential to increase your skills level and thus become a more valuable employee in the future. You can get a GED through your local community college by passing a standardized test; no class work is required.

HOW TO BECOME A COMPUTER TECHNICIAN

Now that you have some idea of what computer technicians do and why they are in such high demand in the job market, let's take a look at how you can join this exciting field. There is no universally accepted way to train for a career in the computer industry because every employer's needs vary with the type of work to be done. Even the traditional *Occupational Outlook Handbook* acknowledges this. There are as many kinds of technicians as there are lakes in Minnesota. With so much variety, you're going to need some help. Read on for step-by-step guidance on becoming a computer technician.

Do you have what it takes to be a computer technician?

Computer technicians must think logically, have good communication skills, and concentrate on a number of tasks simultaneously. Take this brief quiz to determine if a career working with computers is right for you.

Is a career working with computers right for you?	Yes	No
Do you own, or have access to a personal computer?	___	___
Do you enjoy trying out new software packages?	___	___
Have you ever removed the cover from your computer just to see what was inside?	___	___
Have you ever been frustrated by your computer's lack of processing speed and then done something about it?	___	___
Do you enjoy talking to people, even people who disagree with you?	___	___
Do you spend your free time solving problems and puzzles?	___	___
When faced with a subject that you don't understand, do you keep at it until you learn it?	___	___
Do you cope well with change, reacting favorably to it instead of becoming frustrated by it?	___	___
Do you love to learn?	___	___
Do you like to tinker with electronic devices?	___	___
Are you interested in trying to find out how things work?	___	___
Do you currently read any computer industry news?	___	___

If you answered "yes" to several of the questions, chances are you will feel right at home in an industry as challenging and diverse as computer technology. Follow the steps listed in the rest of this chapter to learn what you need to do to become a computer technician.

Get a high school diploma or a GED.

While a career as a computer technician does not always require a college education, high school graduation or a GED *is* required.

- If you're in high school now, there are a number of ways you can prepare for your future career. Take a heavy course schedule; don't neglect the classes that require homework. A career in computers requires good analytical and problem-solving skills; studying math, sciences, and logic will help you attain these skills. If your school offers classes in computers or has a computer lab available to students, take advantage of it. Learn as much about computers as you can. Volunteer in the computer lab and spend your free time learning the operating system (DOS, Windows, or OS2) and as many of the software packages as you can. Familiarity with the computer will help you when you begin the job hunting process.

- If you've recently graduated, you may still be able to make use of your high school's facilities. Discuss your career goals with your school guidance counselor; he or she can help you choose the right level of schooling and obtain financial aid. Deciding on a career path early will allow you to choose the proper course of study and get out into the job market and earning money as soon as possible.

Inventory your computer skills.

If you want to change careers, inventory your computer skills. Do you already have the skills you will need in this new career? Or will you need additional training? In your current job, do you have access to a computer? Are you the one your coworkers come to for help when they have problems with their hardware or software? Does your company link its computers together via LAN (a local area network)? If so, do you understand the technologies used to achieve this link? Are you interested in learning about it? Many people who are changing to a career working with computers will answer these questions in the affirmative. They have made the most of their existing opportunity and are convinced that they will excel as computer technicians. If you don't use a computer in your current occupation and you don't use one at home, you should complete a computer training program before quitting your job.

Learn about the computer industry.

If you are interested in a career as a computer technician, you can begin preparing now by following these simple guidelines offered by an industry expert:

* Take advantage of any opportunity to work with a computer, at home, work, school, or the library. Learn everything you can about how to use it.
* Read about computers and computing professionals in newspapers, books, and magazines. Visit your school or public library. Study the latest trends. Learn about new developments. Read critically, and ask questions about each article. You may not be able to answer those questions now, but you will later.
* Join a computer club at school or in your community. It's a great way to keep up on the latest developments. Members often share software programs and general computing knowledge.
* Talk to people employed in the field. Do you know someone who works with computers? Perhaps he or she will sit down with you for a couple of hours and tell you about the field. Find out the advantages and disadvantages associated with the job. Ask the technician to describe an average day.
* Try to get after-school, part-time, or summer jobs in which you can observe computer specialists at work.

Decide on your area of specialization.

As you'll find when you begin your job search, the term *computer technician* is more than a job title; it's also a set of skills that make you a successful job seeker. Concentrate on one area of specialization and use that knowledge to build your skills in each of the other areas. As noted previously, these are the areas of specialization you will need to consider:

* **Software technicians** have to be good communicators and enjoy working with other people. More non-technical employees use computers every day and often run into computer problems they can't solve. The software technician helps them solve those problems.

- **Hardware technicians** install, maintain, and repair computers and other office equipment. Their responsibilities include installing computers and peripheral devices (printers, drivers, and so on). They also perform routine maintenance and diagnostics.
- **Network technicians** are responsible for the security and administration of corporate networks. Larger companies often employ several network specialists, each of whom performs a different function; smaller companies have one or two people do everything.
- **Internet technicians** manage the corporate Web site and make it possible for the company to access the Internet without putting its corporate security in jeopardy. The most important skill for these technicians is adaptability. As with the entire computer industry, the technology changes rapidly, and the tools you use today will be obsolete tomorrow.

Decide on a mode of training.

Until recently, formal university or vocational courses were not available, and prior work experience was the only "education" required of job applicants. But computer hardware and software change so rapidly that technicians need to update their skills continuously. This training is available from a number of sources, including employers, vendors, colleges and universities, and private training institutions. See chapter two for more information on types of training.

Even though jobs may be available without a formal education, employers do value employees with the initiative to seek continuing education. As in any industry, employers also value experience, but don't let that scare you if you don't have any. Most employers allow some combination of work experience and education, as evidenced in the job posting shown to below:

Wanted:
Electronics Technician–Computer Systems Specialist

Candidate must have

- One year of experience in computer hardware maintenance/installation *OR*
- Six-month certificate of training in computer hardware technology *PLUS* six months of experience in computer hardware maintenance/installation *OR*
- Two-year vocational/technical school program *OR*
- Associate of Arts degree in computer hardware technology

Choose the right school.

Educational opportunities for technicians are increasing in number and variety every year. In years past, only a small number of public and private schools provided training, but recently many colleges are offering this type of occupational training. No matter which training method you ultimately choose, you will have to decide which school is right for you. Chapter three contains a list of training programs that are geared to preparing students for a career working with computers.

Apply to the school of your choice.

Every school's admission requirements will vary, but most will have similar guidelines. They all require some type of formal application or registration process. Each application will have a deadline date and will request basic educational background information and test scores. Some may require an essay explaining your career goals or why you think you should be admitted to the school. Whatever the admission requirements for your school, follow them precisely. If you have any questions about the requirements, don't guess; call the admissions office and find the right answer. You can improve your odds of being admitted by asking questions.

Obtain financial aid.

Once you've decided on the type of training you prefer, you'll need to think about financial aid. Even if you plan to attend classes at a national chain computer store instead of a school, you will probably find some form of financial assistance available to you. Chapter four contains in-depth information on financing the training you need, but here are some quick pointers:

- Don't assume that you won't qualify for some form of aid.
- Make sure you submit your tax forms by April 15.
- Don't lie (or exaggerate) on your application.
- Always submit your applications well within the deadlines.
- Start looking for sources of financial aid as soon as possible.

Graduate from your training program.

Just as your high school diploma is important, the degree, certificate, or knowledge obtained in your training program is vital to your success in this career. Education is the base that will allow you to recognize and understand the changes in the industry. Chapter two will show you how to make the most of your training program.

Prepare your resume.

First impressions count, and your resume is your prospective employer's first chance to learn about you. A good resume convinces the reader that you are qualified for the job and that you are worth interviewing. It is a marketing brochure— you are selling yourself to the employer.

See chapter five for advice and examples to help you create your own resume. Remember to update your resume whenever you have new information to add. If you need to submit your resume in a hurry, you don't want to have to rush to update it—rushing can lead to embarrassing errors.

Decide where you want to work.

Just as you have to make a decision about the type of training you feel most comfortable with, you also need to think about the type of company you'd feel most comfortable in. Computer technicians perform varied job duties, and most companies would like to hire people who can do it all; however, you will find that in most instances, they will hire you based on your expertise in one area.

Large Companies

At large companies, those with more than 500 employees, computer technicians work as a team, and each member of the team has her own specialty. In this way, the company can be assured of having a wealth of knowledge available to them, and the team members are able to concentrate on keeping up with the technology in only one area.

Large companies may be able to provide an additional benefit. Many such companies in metropolitan areas are establishing internship programs. These programs offer students or recent graduates an opportunity to gain experience at little or no cost to the company. Your school's career placement office will be able to help you find companies offering internships, but you also can approach companies yourself. If you decide you want to work at a particular company, call the human resources department and ask if it has an internship program for computer technicians. Even if the answer is no, you may find out where to address a formal inquiry. You will have to propose the program, explain how it benefits both parties, and set a time limit.

Small Companies

Companies with fewer than 100 employees will usually hire an individual who has expertise in one technical area but will require that he or she learn other areas. For instance, the company may be experiencing rapid growth and decide it's ready to hire a network technician. So it does, but the individual hired will be responsible for learning about software and Internet technologies too.

Universities

Like large companies, universities and colleges will typically hire individuals with expertise in a single area of technology. They differ in the type of technology used; businesses generally operate on PC client-server technology, while universities also use mainframes.

Government Agencies

Government agencies also use both client-server technology and mainframes. However, they have the added security requirements you might expect. They want to hire people with technical experience in support and a knowledge of security procedures.

Contract Agencies

Contract agencies offer an interesting opportunity for technicians. Many companies are finding that they need technicians to perform a specific job for a limited amount of

> **Wanted:**
> **Computer Technicians**
>
> We are looking for qualified laptop and desktop repair technicians with a minimum of one to two years of experience in Compaq, IBM, Apple, Packard-Bell, AST, NEC, etc. Responsible for troubleshooting, repairing, and testing. Must be able to upgrade hardware and software and have knowledge of DOS, Windows, and utilities programs.

time. For example, suppose a company with a staff of competent technicians decides to install a new network. The company's own technicians are perfectly capable of maintaining the new system but would require a great deal of training to be able to design and install the new system. That company may decide that it makes sense to *temporarily* contract with a technician who has the skills necessary to set up the new system.

Find the right job.

After you know the type of job you want and the type of company you want to work for and have prepared your resume, it's time to find the job that's right for you. See chapter five for a wealth of tips for conducting a successful job search.

THE INSIDE TRACK

Who:	John David
What:	Technical support manager
Where:	Tennessee
How much:	$58,000 per year

Insider's Advice

This type of work (technical support) used to be performed only by electricians and required a basic background in electricity and electronics, with knowledge of transistors, capacitors, diodes, integrated circuits, chips, etc. Technology has changed so much that with minimal training and a thorough understanding of networking anyone can get started as a computer technician in most companies.

Most equipment manufacturers offer training, and once you have secured a job, the company usually will train you on the new equipment in its facility or send you to the manufacturer for training. Possibly the best opportunity today for a novice is to attend a computer-specific technical college to get the basics. It's important to look for one that has a high job-placement record.

Anyone interested in working in this field must be willing to learn new equipment and technologies continually. It is a very fast paced, high-pressure, multitasking, self-starter type of job. Even if you get your foot in the door at a company and start working, you will be amazed and how much more you have to learn.

Insider's Take on the Future

The technician's job is constantly changing. The equipment you have today will be obsolete in a year or two. But it is exciting and very satisfying when you have the knowledge and skill to keep a system or network running at peak performance. I am constantly looking for training classes and reading the industry magazines—I don't think that will change in the near future.

CHAPTER 2

This chapter explains the training you need to become a computer technician. You'll find tips on how to evaluate training programs and several sample course descriptions from training programs across the country, so you can get an idea of the types of programs and classes offered for each job. Then you'll get advice on studying for exams, taking notes, networking with class-mates, and getting to know your instructor.

ALL ABOUT TRAINING PROGRAMS

Although you may be able to get a job as a computer technician without formal training right now, that won't always be the case. As with any job in an emerging field, you may be able to get in without training while the field is still being defined. But training programs will spring up to meet industry needs.

WHY SHOULD YOU GET TRAINING?

The Competitive Job Market

With many training programs in place, the computer technician without formal training will be at a disadvantage for two reasons. First, you will be competing against many technicians who have formal training. Second, once the market has many skilled employees with formal training, compa-nies will start mandating that all technicians have a degree or certificate. Your formal training—whether you pursue a two-year degree or a certificate that you can complete in a few weeks or months—plus your experience will keep you competitive in your field for the years to come.

Natural Talent Myth

You may think you don't need formal training and say to yourself, "I know how to use a computer."

And in fact you may be quite proficient at using your computer. But knowing how to use it does not translate into knowing how to fix it or how to configure it. You probably also know how to drive a car, but who is going to ask you to overhaul the transmission in their car?

You even may have figured out how to configure, fix, and upgrade your computer through trial and error. Unfortunately, trial and error methods do not give you an effective intellectual toolkit and problem-solving skills. You know how to do a limited number of things, and you only know one way to do them. A formal training program will equip you with a global perspective on computer systems; you will understand the relationships between the components of the system, and you will know a variety of ways to address each situation.

The Movie Myth

Don't believe everything you see on the big screen. The movies about people working in the computer industry are just not realistic. Computers are made of hardware and software. They are useful in business, school, and home. They cannot be used by any Joe and Jane off the street to take over the entire city of New York in an hour. While movies are exciting and entertaining, you will not get an accurate picture of the computer industry from them. You need trusted, proven, down-to-earth training from a reputable source.

HOW TO EVALUATE TRAINING PROGRAMS

Schools are businesses; they need students in order to make money. When you think of it in that light, the brochure you read about a school is actually advertising. You, as a consumer, need to carefully research, evaluate, and compare schools the same way you would if you were buying a stereo.

You need a list of criteria for judging the school's worth to you. For instance, do you want to attend school full time or part time? Are you more comfortable in a rural or urban setting? What kind of student-teacher ratio are you looking for?

All of this information is available through a number of sources, including the schools themselves. Make a chart like the one below to help you compare the choices and make your decision.

Selecting A School				
My Criteria	**School A**	**School B**	**School C**	**School D**
Rural setting	X	X		
Public school	X	X	X	X
Computer lab open 24 hours	X			X
Computer lab has PC and UNIX platforms	X		X	
Computer lab hires students	X			X
Student body size less than 10,000		X		X
Student-to-teacher ratio less than 10 to1		X		X
Coed campus	X	X	X	X
Financial aid offered through the school			X	
Work-study program available	X	X	X	X
On-campus placement office	X	X		X
Large nontraditional student population			X	

If you have time, try to visit the schools in your area and talk to the guidance counselor. These counselors are trained to help you identify your needs and decide if their school will meet your criteria. Follow this checklist in preparing for an on-campus visit:

- Contact the office of admissions to request an appointment to visit. Remember to ask for the name of the person making the appointment and the person you will be meeting with.
- Bring a copy of your transcript or permanent record card if you will have the opportunity to meet with an admissions counselor during your visit.
- Include a list of honors or awards you have received in school or the community.
- Know your PSAT and ACT or SAT test scores in case someone asks you about them.

♦ Be ready to ask questions about the school and surrounding community, especially about extracurricular activities and work opportunities and other details you won't find in the promotional brochures.

Questions to Ask About Training Programs
Is the Program Accredited?
The accreditation process recognizes schools and professional programs that provide a level of performance, integrity, and quality to its students and the community. The accreditation process is voluntary; accreditation is granted on the basis of the school's curriculum, staff ratios, and other criteria established by the accrediting agencies. Accreditation doesn't attempt to rank or grade the schools, only to accredit them.

So what does that mean to you? Basically, it assures you, *and your potential employers*, that the school you chose to attend provides valuable courses taught by qualified instructors. In short, it offers you peace of mind.

Three national accreditation agencies and six regional agencies have jurisdiction over the entire United States; schools can also be accredited by professional organizations. Though a school can be accredited by more than one agency, one is enough. Most schools are proud of their accredited status and freely share the information in their printed materials, but you can be sure of their status by asking. Be sure that all programs you evaluate are accredited by one of the accrediting bodies listed in Appendix A.

What is the Program's Length?
You have choices about the amount of time you spend on your training. The section Length of Training Programs later in this chapter provides a description and comparison of the length of programs and courses. Decide in advance how long you want to spend on your training and find a program that meets your needs and budget.

What is the Student-Teacher Ratio?
The student-teacher ratio is a statistic that shows the average number of students assigned to one teacher in a classroom or lab. It is important to know the ratio because a lower student-teacher ratio means that, as a student, you will get more small-group, one-on-one, intense training. A higher ratio (30 to 1 or even 100 to 1) is sometimes acceptable for a lecture class in which interaction between

students and teachers is not necessary. However, for a lab setting (hands-on work), students need a lower student-teacher ratio: 30 to 1 might be acceptable for easy work, 15 to 1 for moderate projects; intense work might require a 5 to 1 or even 1 to 1 ratio.

What is the Classroom-Lab Ratio?

Theory and discussion, which you will get in a classroom setting, are important. However, lab experience—working with hardware and software, hands-on—is equally important in a technical degree program. Evaluate how much of your training time will be spent in the classroom versus the lab. Be cautious about any program that does not include significant lab work.

Is the School's Lab Technologically Advanced?

Technology is changing rapidly; it would be a waste to have excellent student-teacher ratios in a lab full of old technology. While it is important to be familiar with hardware and software that is a few years old (your future employer probably has some old equipment), you need to be sure that you will also have experience working with state-of-the-art equipment. Investigate how the labs in your prospective schools are equipped, maintained, and updated.

What are the School's Job-Placement Statistics?

Most schools and programs have specific placement offices, dedicated to helping you find a job after you have completed your training. Placement offices keep records of what types of jobs their students get. Don't just read the statistics; closely examine them. Understand the difference between a statistic that shows how many students got jobs in the computer field and one that shows how many got jobs, even in unrelated fields. Find out how many jobs were found through the placement office and how many students found jobs independently. Even if the school does not have a job placement service, you still should be able find out what percent of graduating students find jobs in the computer industry.

Does the School Offer Internships?

An internship, a source of experience and potential employment, is an excellent opportunity for any student. In an internship, a student works in a company for a short time (often one to three months) to complete a predefined project or task. The students are paid an internship salary, which is usually low, or are not paid a salary at all. But internships are valuable because they offer on-the-job experience, a chance to create portfolio pieces, and opportunities to network with other people in the field. And many internships turn into full-time positions with the interning company. Find out if any of your prospective programs or schools have internships with companies in the area.

Entrance Requirements

Depending on which program and school you choose to attend, you may have to complete entrance and placement exams. These exams evaluate your reading, writing, and math skills. For example, if you score low in math on a placement exam, you may be placed in a remedial math course such as Math 099 to use as review before taking Math 101. Other criteria used in admitting applicants to programs include high school grade point average, recommendations, and personal statements.

Length of Training Programs

Training programs in the computer industry range from single courses to advanced degrees. So how do you determine which path is best for you? Here are some things to consider:

- The more education you have, the better your opportunities for getting a job.
- The more education you have, the better your opportunities for advancing into supervisory or management positions.
- You don't want to become a professional student. You want to fulfill an educational goal, and then you want to get a job to fulfill career and financial goals.
- You must be realistic about your present financial situation. You probably can get financial aid or loans to go through school, but you also must consider rent, food, and those who need your financial support.

You will find three basic types of education: course certification, program certification, and degrees.

Type of Education	Description	Typical Time	Where to Get the Training
Course certification	A class that focuses on one piece of software or one technology.	Ranges from half a day to six months	Temporary agencies Private training companies Vendors (the companies that make hardware or software or other technologies)
Program certification	A series of classes that give an overview of a field.	One to two years	Vocational schools Proprietary schools Independent colleges Technical schools
Associate degree	Two years of college-level work, with courses in general education and specialized studies.	Two years	Colleges Universities Technical Schools
Bachelor's degree	Four years of college-level work, with courses in general education and a specialized major subject.	Four years	Colleges Universities

TYPES OF TRAINING COURSES

Most computer technician jobs do not require a four-year college degree. In fact, courses at traditional four-year schools focus primarily on programming, not on operations, maintenance, or networking. Computer technician courses are offered more often through two-year colleges, technical schools, and proprietary facilities (private teaching facilities, sometimes run by a vendor). Though not a complete list, the courses described below will give you an idea of the type of training you can expect to find in a training program near you.

Sample Courses
Network Technician

Here are some typical courses for preparing to become a network technician.

Network Operating Systems

Courses with this title familiarize the student with popular network operating systems including Novell NetWare® and Microsoft Windows NT®.

Networking Essentials

Current networking technologies for local area networks (LAN), metropolitan area networks (MAN), wide area networks (WAN), and the Internet. In addition to understanding the configuration requirements for these networks, you will also learn system administration techniques.

Network Design

Learn about designing complex networks, the directory structure and naming conventions, partition/replica strategies, remote user configuration, and techniques for project management.

Certified Novell Engineer (CNE) Training

Following the structure of the certification test, this course prepares the student to pass the exam. It includes training on Novell NetWare® installation; configuration; TCP/IP transport; Ethernet, Arcnet, and Token Ring configurations; and Novell system administration guidelines.

Hardware Technician

Here are some typical courses for preparing to become a hardware technician.

Computer Hardware and Small Computer Systems

An introduction to the design and operation of small computer systems (PC clones), this course emphasizes logic circuit design and basic assembly language programming.

Supporting Operating Systems

This course teaches skills for handling day-to-day administration and technical support of various operating systems.

Introduction to the Psychology of Computer Support

This course teaches methods for coping with stress, communicating with both the people you support and your supervisors, and purchasing replacement parts.

Software Technician

Here are some typical courses for preparing to become a software technician.

Microsoft Office User Specialist

Designed to validate skills in using Microsoft Office, the certification that accompanies this program positions you to provide excellent support for the Microsoft Office suite. Students learn how to support the Microsoft Word, Excel, PowerPoint, Access, and Outlook programs used in almost 90 percent of Fortune 500 companies.

Supporting Microsoft Word for Windows

Intended for technical support specialists, this four-day course teaches students to install the software locally or on a network; customize user environments; organize document file structure; customize templates; and share information with other programs.

Supporting Microsoft Windows

A five-day course designed to enable technicians to install, configure, support, and troubleshoot Microsoft Windows. The course describes maintenance and troubleshooting tools, communications and networking protocols, and hardware support.

Internet Technician

Here are some typical courses for preparing to become an Internet technician.

Understanding the Internet

Students learn about the transmission control protocol/Internet protocol (TCP/IP) and how to install a TCP/IP stack on a network.

Web Basics

Students learn how to support the hardware and peripherals required to maintain a successful Web site and how to choose the right Internet service provider (ISP) for any Web needs.

Internet Security

Students learn to identify possible security risks imposed by the Internet and how to avoid them. Corporate firewalls and file permissions are explained.

Academic and Vendor-Affiliated Training Programs

You can receive academic training through an accredited school, college, or university; this type of training provides you with a broad scope of information about many elements of computers made by many different vendors. This book contains information about two-year degrees, generally called associate degrees, and vendor training, generally called certification. Vendor certification provides intense training on all the products made by one company (such as Microsoft, Novell, or Lotus). Some academic programs also provide vendor training as a part of their degree program. Because computer technology is growing, the opportunities for training are increasing rapidly.

Academic Computer Training Programs

Because computer technology is still a relatively new field, most schools have their own naming conventions for programs; there are no universal terms used to name academic computer programs. You rarely will find a program called Computer Technician, but there are a lot of closely related titles. Most programs offer essentially the same information—you will find many similar courses even under different program titles. Here are just some of the names used for programs related to the computer technician field. The training programs listed in the directory in chapter three use these titles or similar ones:

- Computer Business Systems Technology
- Computer Electro-Mechanics
- Computer Engineering Technology
- Computer Hardware Technology
- Computer Information Science
- Computer Information Systems
- Computer Information Systems Management
- Computer Information Systems Technology
- Computer Literacy
- Computer Maintenance
- Computer Maintenance Technology
- Computer Management Systems
- Computer Networking
- Computer Operations
- Computer Repair
- Computer Science
- Computer Science and Business
- Computer Science and Electronics
- Computer Science and Information Studies
- Computer Services Theory and Systems
- Computer Systems Technology
- Computer Technology

The best approach is to contact schools and ask for a catalog of their courses related to the computer field. Then you can see for yourself which of their courses are related to becoming specifically, a hardware technician, software technician, network technician, or Internet technician. You can also call the schools that interest you and speak to an admissions counselor for more detailed information.

Below are two samples of academic training schools that have several branches across the nation offering training for computer technicians.

DeVry Technical Institute

DeVry provides academic programs that unite education, technology, and business. The school offers two different programs for training computer technicians: Computer Information Systems and Electronics Technician. See the Directory of Academic Computer Training Programs in chapter three to see if there is a school near you. You can register for classes or get more information online at *http://www.devry.com.*

ITT Technical Institute

ITT Technical Institute provides academic programs that unite education, technology, and business. It offers training for computer technicians in its Electronics Technician program. ITT Technical Institute has over 50 schools across the nation. See the Directory of Academic Computer Training Programs in chapter three for a school near you.

Tips on Applying to Academic Programs

- Apply as early as you can. You'll need to fill out an application and submit official high school or GED transcripts and any copies of SAT, ACT, or other test scores used for admission. If you haven't taken these, you may have to before you can be admitted. Call the school and find out when the next programs starts, and then apply at least a month or two prior to make sure you can complete requirements before the program starts.

- You may receive a prewritten request for transcripts from the admissions office when you get your application. Make sure you respond promptly so you don't hold up the admissions process.

- Make an appointment as soon as possible to take placement tests if they are required.

- Pay your fees before the deadline. Enrollment is not complete each quarter or semester until you have paid all fees by the date specified on the registration form. If fees are not paid by the deadline, your classes may be canceled. If you are going to receive financial aid, apply as early as you can.

- Find out if you must pass a physical or have any other medical history forms on file for the school you choose, so this does not delay your admission.

Vendor-Affiliated Computer Training Programs

Vendors are companies that make specific products. Several training companies are affiliated with one or more vendors and are authorized to teach their curriculum. This section discusses the most popular and widely obtained certifications in the computer industry: Microsoft, Novell, Lotus, and A+. Read on for more details about how to obtain the training you need to pass certification exams in these exciting areas.

Microsoft Certification

Microsoft offers five certifications:

- Microsoft certified systems engineer
- Microsoft certified solutions developer
- Microsoft certified professional
- Microsoft certified trainer
- Microsoft certified professional, specialist: Internet

You can get training in a classroom or through self-paced training.

Instructor-led classroom training	Hands-on technical training is available from Microsoft Authorized Academic Training Programs (AATP) and Microsoft Authorized Technical Education Centers (ATEC).
Self-paced training	Self-paced training is available in a variety of formats, including books, training kits, videos, computer-based media, and broadcast programs.

Acquiring Microsoft certification status can increase job opportunities. Certification is available from two types of authorized trainers:

- Authorized Academic Training Programs (AATP)
- Authorized Technical Education Centers (ATEC)

Authorized Academic Training Programs (AATP)

Students can find instructor-led training on Microsoft products and technologies through high schools, colleges, and universities participating in the Microsoft Authorized Academic Training Program (AATP). The curriculum is developed by Microsoft and prepares students for certification exams.

AATP institutions deliver Microsoft Official Curriculum (MOC) in a conventional classroom setting. Developed by Microsoft, MOC courses provide a hands-on experience, with lectures, labs, and supplemental materials. You can contact Microsoft at 800-508-8454 to find out if participating AATP institutions are located near you.

Authorized Technical Education Centers (ATEC)

Microsoft Authorized Technical Education Centers (ATEC) offer several training options. Companies (generally private companies) that are Microsoft Certified Solutions Providers prepare students for taking certification exams. These programs are shorter than the academic associate degree programs, and some courses can be completed within a few days or weeks. See the Directory of Vendor-Affiliated Computer Training Programs in chapter three for a sampling of centers near you.

Novell Certification

Novell offers the following certifications:

- Certified Novell salesperson (CNS)
- Certified Novell administrator (CNA)
- Certified Novell engineer (CNE)
- Master CNE
- Certified Novell instructor (CNI)

Acquiring Novell certification status can increase job opportunities. Certification is available from two types of authorized trainers:

- Novell Authorized Education Center (NAEC)
- Novell Education Academic Partner (NEAP)

Novell Authorized Education Centers (NAEC)

Novell Authorized Education Centers (NAEC) offer several training options. Private companies are authorized by Novell to provide Novell training to students preparing to take certification exams. These programs are shorter than the academic associate degree programs, and some courses can be completed within a few days or weeks. See the Directory of Vendor-Affiliated Computer Training Programs in chapter three for schools near you.

Novell Education Academic Partner (NEAP)

Students can find instructor-led training on Novell products and technologies through high schools, colleges, and universities participating in the Novell Education Academic Partner program. The curriculum is developed by Novell and prepares students for certification exams.

Curriculum developed by Novell is delivered in a conventional classroom setting; the courses provide a hands-on experience, with lectures, labs, and supplemental materials. Call your local community or technical college to see if it offers Novell certification training.

Lotus Certification

Lotus offers the following certifications:

- Application developer
- Principal application developer
- System administrator
- Principal system administrator
- Lotus cc:mail certification
- Cc:mail specialist
- Instructor certification

You can seek professional certification by attending Lotus authorized, instructor-led courses or completing Lotus self-paced computer-based training courses. For more information about Lotus training and to find a Lotus training program near you, call the Lotus education helpline at 800-346-6409 or 617-693-4436.

A+ Certification

A+ Certification is a home-study program. To become certified, you must pass two test modules: the Core and the Windows/DOS modules. Candidates who pass the two test modules become certified, demonstrating basic knowledge of configuring, installing, diagnosing, repairing, upgrading, and maintaining microcomputers and associated technologies.

The course is in an interactive, Windows-based format that lets you practice answering questions as if you were taking the actual test. The A+ course includes:

- The *A+ Certification Success Guide* for computer technicians
- Interactive certification assessment software

+ Over 900 sample questions on three disks
+ A study guide and workbook

You can order the A+ course online (*http://www.lantell.org/form.htm*) or register for the A+ by calling 800-776-4276. Tests are given at Sylvan Prometric Authorized Test Centers.

Sample Computer Training Programs

These programs are listed as examples only. School curriculums are subject to change at any time.

Program Name	Associate in Applied Science		
Location	New River Community College		
Program Length	2 years		
Semester 1	**Semester 2**	**Semester 3**	**Semester 4**
DC Fundamentals	Math for Liberal Arts 1	Programming C	Local Area Networks
Intro to Computing	Database Management	Programming COBOL	Programming Basic
Supervised Lab	Technical Writing	Social Science	Microcomputers
Pre-Calculus	Electronic Devices 1	Health/Phys Ed	Oral Communication
Orientation	AC Fundamentals	Elective	Social Science
	Health/Phys Ed		

Program Name	Associate in Applied Science		
Location	Northern Virginia Community College		
Program Length	2 years		
Semester 1	**Semester 2**	**Semester 3**	**Semester 4**
College Composition	Technical Writing	Communications	Technical Physics
Basic Programming	AC Fundamentals	Intermediate Electronics	Communications 2
DC Fundamentals	Devices and Application	Microprocessor	Digital Communications
Technical Math	Logic Circuits	Adv Eng Tech Math	Interpersonal Skills
Social Science	Technical Math 2	Elective	Social Science
Lifetime Fitness			
Elective			

Program Name Computer Technology Specialization

Location Northern Virginia Community College

Program Length 2 years

Semester 1	Semester 2	Semester 3	Semester 4
College Composition	Technical Writing	Intermediate Electronics	Electronic Controls
Basic Programming	AC Fundamentals	Microprocessor App	Microprocessor App 2
DC Fundamentals	Devices and Application	Technical Physics	Computer Interfacing
Technical Math	Logic Circuits	Interpersonal Skills	Digital Communications
Social Science	Technical Math 2	Social Science	RPK
Lifetime Fitness			
Orientation			

Program Name Business Equipment/Computer Technician

Location Idaho State University

Program Length 1 1/2 years

Semester 1	Semester 2	Semester 3
Academic Skills Dev	Basic Electronics	Product Sales
Typewriters	Electronic Cash	Basic Computing Servicing
Keyboarding/OS	Register Calculator	Special Topics
Customer Relations	Bond Copier/Laser Printer	Applied Communications
Basic Electrical Theory		Applied Occ Relations

Program Name Microsoft Certified Systems Engineer

Location Various locations nationwide or home study

Program Length Self-paced

Required	Any two of the following are required	Electives
Implementing and Supporting Microsoft® Windows NT® Server 4.0	Microsoft® Windows® 3.1	Plus two electives
	Microsoft® Windows® for Workgroups 3.11	
Implementing and Supporting Microsoft® Windows NT® Server 4.0 in the Enterprise	Implementing and Supporting Microsoft® Windows® 95	
	Implementing and Supporting Microsoft® Windows® 95	
	Implementing and Supporting Microsoft® Windows NT® Workstation 4.0	

Program Name	Certified Novell Engineer in NetWare 3	
Location	Various locations nationwide	
Program Length	Self-paced, but it's recommended that you finish within a year	
Required for all CNE programs	**Required for the NetWare 3 program**	**Electives**
Networking Technologies	NetWare 3.1x Administration	Plus two
Service and Support Test	NetWare 3.1x Advanced Administration	electives
	NetWare 3 Installation & Configuration Workshop	
	IntranetWare: NetWare 3 to NetWare 4.11 Update	

You may find that a combination of courses and programs works best for you. For example, you may decide to get a two-year associate degree in computer technology so you'll have a good general background, and then take a couple of certification courses to specialize in one or more areas. Here's what Eckhart Boehme, marketing manager of the Microsoft Certified Professional Program, has to say about the value of getting Microsoft certification:

> Microsoft certification credentials are awarded to individuals who have successfully demonstrated their ability to perform specific tasks and implement solutions with Microsoft products. Through certification, computer professionals can maximize the return on their investment in Microsoft technology. Research shows that Microsoft certification provides organizations with increased customer satisfaction and decreased support costs through improved service, increased productivity, and greater technical self-sufficiency; a reliable benchmark for hiring, promoting, and career planning; recognition and rewards for productive employees by validating their expertise; and retraining options for existing employees so they can work effectively with new technologies.

HOW TO MAKE THE MOST OF YOUR TRAINING PROGRAM

After you decide to enter a training program to receive a certificate or degree, you want to make the most of it, right? The rest of this chapter shows you how to do just that by providing specific things you can do to maximize the benefits of completing your training program.

Taking Notes in Class

Very few people are gifted with a photographic memory that allows them to remember all the information that bombards them throughout the day. And very few students are gifted with a lightning-quick hand that can record everything said in a classroom. So it is essential to your success in a training course that you use an effective note-taking method that will help you learn and remember key information.

Note-Taking Methods

There are basically three different kinds of note-taking. You should give a few trial runs to each to discover which one fits your learning style best.

Traditional Outline

The traditional outline method is typically the basis for teachers' lectures. Concepts (broad ideas) are farthest left, marked by Roman numerals (I, II, III); the ideas and details that expand the concept are marked first by capital letters (A, B, C), then Arabic numbers (1, 2, 3), then lowercase letters (a, b, c). Increase the indent with each level of detail.

You don't have to get all the lettering and numbering exactly correct. The important part of this method is to understand and accurately record the relationships between ideas (for example, this idea is really a subset of that idea). Here is a sample of this method:

> I. How to make the most of your training program
>> A. Taking notes in class
>>> 1. Methods
>>>> a. Outline
>>>> b. Columns
>>>> c. Diagramming
>>> 2. Shorthand
>> B. Studying for exams
> II. Finding training

Three-Column Method

The three-column method is basically a more artistic way of outlining. The advantages over outlining are:

- You don't have to spend time writing down roman numerals and numbers and worrying about correct indents, so you will be able to write faster.
- You don't have to understand the exact relationships of less important concepts at the time they are presented.
- Some people are visual learners, and this method works better for them. Be prepared to use a lot of paper this way; your third column fills up fast.

Making the most of training	Methods for taking notes	Outline
		Column
		Diagram
		Shorthand
	Methods for studying	List your methods here
Finding training		

Informal Diagramming

Informal diagramming allows your imagination to run wild while still sticking to the facts of the matter. You choose how to represent the main idea and how to make the details feed into that. This can be very useful for "how-to" type information about computers, because it's essentially a flowchart, a common method of presenting information in the technology industry. Creating different ways to visually represent relationships helps you to analyze and synthesize the information, leading to greater comprehension. And exercising your artistic side will help keep you awake in class! (It's a great alternative to doodling.)

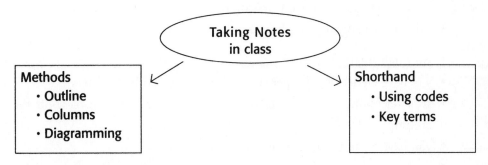

Invent Your Own Shorthand

Even when you find the right note-taking method for your learning style, getting down every word an instructor speaks is virtually impossible. Don't attempt this with a laptop, even if your typing skills are top-notch: you'll be miserable trying to condense and organize the material after class. You need to invent ways to abbreviate words. Constantly writing out "computer" and "because" and "training" is time-consuming (and your wrist will protest). You can write *bc* for *because*. So many words end with *-ing*, why not just add *-g*? The common ending *-tion* can become *-tn*. And drop as many vowels as possible without making the word indecipherable. For example, *training* can easily become *trng*. Use acronyms (just the first letter of each word) for key terms that are repeated over and over. How many times could you write *c.t.* for each time you spell out *computer technician*?

You rarely need to write complete sentences. The meat of a sentence is its noun and verb—skip all the extra words (like *the*, and *it*).

If you haven't tried it before, creating your own shorthand is going to involve trial and error, just like any other note-taking method. It's not important that everyone else understands your notes, only that *you* understand them.

Review Your Notes

Look over your notes as soon as possible after class—within twelve hours. Fill in any missing information you still remember; cross out what obviously became unimportant by the time the class was over. Mark key points with a highlighter. Make sure each set of notes is clearly titled with date, course title, teacher's name, and overall theme.

Studying for Exams

Try to budget your study time so you don't have to cram for an exam. Pulling an all-nighter is *not* a red badge of courage in education. Studies show that you will study less effectively and perform worse on tests when you are tired.

Set up a reasonably neat study area and make sure:

+ your lighting is good
+ you have plenty of pens, pencils, Post-It notes, and highlighters
+ your telephone isn't going to ring with a tempting offer to blow off the evening
+ you have a comfortable chair and posture
+ you're not going to be distracted by lyrics or awesome bass if you enjoy listening to music while you study

Of course, your notes are already in order, well-titled, clear, and concise. You've also been using your handy highlighter in the textbooks to capture key information, right?

Ask your instructor about the exam format: essay, multiple choice, lab, or one of the many other methods of testing. You probably won't take many essay exams in your coursework; you probably will encounter a lot of multiple-choice and lab (hands-on) tests.

Networking with Other Students

It can be lonely out there, so why not make friends on campus? Observe who is in more than one of your classes; those students probably share some of your goals and interests. Compare your courses of study and ask about their plans after they finish their training. Note announcements of get-togethers organized by major field of study, and attend with a friendly attitude. This may help you become aware of students who are in the same boat with you, even if you didn't notice them before. Getting used to networking with other students will help prepare you for networking to find a job after you complete your training program.

Getting to Know Your Instructors

It is important to have peers for moral support and fun, but it's just as important to get to know your instructors. Being just a number to them will do you no more good than taking a correspondence course. When they know you personally, chances are you will learn more from their class. You can approach them with questions that are too time-consuming or off the main subject to ask in class. You will discover that they are flesh and blood, not just robotic dispensers of knowledge, and knowing this will enrich your educational experience. After your class has met once or twice, find out your instructors' schedules and office location. Make a point to drop by the office at least twice a month, even if it's just to chat about how things are going for you. Look for notices from student organizations announcing special social times to gather with instructors. Remember, they were students once too.

Making the Most of Your Career Placement/Counseling Office

There are squadrons of people out there who have made it *their* job to run career placement and counseling offices just for the students on campus. That includes you. Don't shun their efforts. Make the office one of the first places you visit when you set foot on campus, and include it on your list as you're making rounds to the instructors' offices. Read the posters and notices on the walls. Start by asking general questions to get a feel for the office. Focus on interacting with one particular person so you aren't just a number—just as you do with your instructors. If one staff person takes an interest in your situation, he or she will be able to give you more personalized help and more detailed information.

Not every placement office works the same way. Most offices participate in career fairs and distribute candidate position lists. Career fairs are generally held in large buildings such as hotels or convention centers. They are a great opportunity to learn more about companies in the field and trends in the marketplace, get experience interviewing, and find a job.

THE INSIDE TRACK

Who:	Jeffrey Lyle
What:	Computer support technician
Where:	Minnesota
How much:	$42,000 annual salary

Insider's Advice

Education gives you a knowledge base to grow from, and the bigger and broader that base, the faster you will become productive in the workplace and the higher you will advance within your field. There is no substitute, though, for hands-on experience and dealing with real problems and situations.

Anyone interested in becoming a computer technician should have a genuine interest in the field because it requires continuing effort and education to keep up with the changes and be successful. Computer hardware and software change so rapidly that what was learned two years ago may not apply today.

Insider's Take on the Future

I'm very excited about my job right now. Our company is growing so fast that we have added two new support technicians, and I am going to get a chance to focus on Internet support. It's a whole new area for me and promises to be very challenging. I love learning about new technologies and can't wait to try something new.

CHAPTER | 3

This chapter contains a directory of technical and career schools, proprietary and vocational schools, independent colleges, and other schools that offer training programs for the computer technician jobs discussed in this book. All programs provide school name, address, and phone number, so you can contact each school directly to get more information and application forms for the programs that interest you.

DIRECTORY OF COMPUTER TRAINING PROGRAMS

Now that you've decided to get into a training program, you need to know which schools are available near you. This chapter contains information about two main categories of training: academic programs and vendor-affiliated programs (including Microsoft and Novell certification programs). The academic programs listed in this chapter are offered by technical schools and colleges, and the vendor training programs are offered by private companies or career schools. There are three lists of vendor-affiliated programs. The first includes schools that offer both Microsoft and Novell certification training; the second, schools that offer Microsoft certification training; and the third, schools that offer Novell certification training. The schools are listed in alphabetical order by city and state within each list, so you can quickly locate schools near you. Keep in mind that the schools listed may offer additional certification training at select locations, so it's best to contact each school for a complete and current list of their offerings. The specific schools included in this chapter are not endorsed or recommended by LearningExpress, and not all schools that offer computer training programs are listed here due to space limitations. But the representative listings for each state will help you begin your search for an appropriate school. In addition to the several independent colleges and technical schools listed in this directory, many community colleges offer computer technician training programs, so check your local yellow pages for a listing of community colleges near you. Also, see Appendix A for names of professional associations from which you can request additional lists of accredited and/or authorized training programs in your area.

DIRECTORY OF ACADEMIC COMPUTER TRAINING PROGRAMS

Many of these programs offer computer technician training under a variety of program titles, such as computer hardware technology, computer information systems technology, computer information science, and so on. Therefore, when you contact schools you are interested in, be sure to request information about all the computer programs they offer, regardless of specific program title. See chapter two for a list of the possible program titles and for sample courses related to computer technician jobs.

ALABAMA
Sparks State Technical College
Hwy. 431 S.
Eufaula 36027
334-687-3543; 800-543-2426

Drake State Technical College
34321 Meridian St.
Huntsville 35811
205-539-8161 x110

Southeast College of Technology
A Subsidiary of Education America, Inc.
828 Downtowner Loop W.
Mobile 36609
205-343-8200

Hobson State Technical College
P.O. Box 489
Thomasville 36784
205-636-9642

ALASKA
New Frontier Vocational Training Center
P.O. Box 1869
Soldotna 99669
907-262-9055

ARIZONA
DeVry Institute of Technology
2149 W. Dunlop Ave.
Phoenix 85021-2995
602-870-9222; 800-528-0250

High-Tech Institute
1515 East Indian School Rd.
Phoenix 85014
602-279-9700; 800-832-4011

ITT Technical Institute
1840 East Benson Hwy.
Tucson 85714
602-294-2944

ARKANSAS

Crowley's Ridge Technical Institute
P.O. Box 925
Forrest City 72336-0925
501-633-5411; 800-842-2317

ITT Technical Institute
4520 S. University Ave.
Little Rock 72204
501-565-5550

Southern Technical College of Little Rock
7601 Scott Hamlin Dr.
Little Rock 72209
501-663-6699

Northwest Technical Institute
P.O. Drawer A
Springdale 72765-1301
501-751-8824

CALIFORNIA

Alameda Computer Center
2415 Mariner Sq. Dr., Suite 104
Alameda 94501
510-865-9985; 800-404-9986

Associated Technical College
1177 N. Magnolia Ave.
Anaheim 92801
714-229-8785

Practical Schools
900 East Ball Rd.
Anaheim 92805
714-535-6000; 800-634-8260

Computer Institute
P.O. Box 4352
Culver City 90230
310-822-8035

Advanced Computer Training School
3467 West Shaw Ave., Suite 100
Fresno 93711
209-277-1900

National Training Institute
1788 North Helm, Rm. 105
Fresno 93710
209-456-1522

Institute of Computer Technology
3200 Wilshire Blvd.
Los Angeles 90010
213-381-3333

Los Angeles Trade-Technical College
400 West Washington Blvd.
Los Angeles 90015
213-744-9000

Technical School, Inc.
1638 W. 8th St., Suite 321
Los Angeles 90017
213-386-2879

Ameritech Colleges
5445 Lankershim Blvd.
North Hollywood 91601
818-901-7311; 800-734-4733

DeVry Institute of Technology
901 Corporate Center Dr.
Pomona 91768-2642
909-622-9800

Advanced Career Technologies Institute
2880 Sunset Blvd., Suite 232
Rancho Cordova 95742
916-635-3435

Advance Computer Institute
804 E. Cypress Ave., # D
Redding 96002
916-222-6701

American Technical College for Career Training
191 South E St.
San Bernadino 92401
909-885-3857

COLORADO
Barnes Business College
150 Sheridan Blvd.
Denver 80226
303-922-8454; 800-933-2989

Denver Technical College
925 S. Niagara St.
Denver 80224
303-329-3000

Denver Technical College
225 South Union
Colorado Springs 80910
719-632-3000

CONNECTICUT
Porter and Chester Institute
125 Silas Deane Hwy.
Wethersfield 06109
203-529-2519; 800-870-6789

DISTRICT OF COLUMBIA
NRI Schools
4401 Connecticut Ave. NW
Washington 20008
202-244-1600

FLORIDA
Florida Atlantic University
777 Glades Rd., P.O. Box 3091
Boca Raton 33431-0991
561-367-3258; FAX: 561-367-3987

ATI Career Training Center
2880 NW 62nd St.
Ft. Lauderdale 33309
954-973-4760; 800-388-8663

Florida Technical College
8711 Lone Star Rd.
Jacksonville 32211
904-724-2229

ATI Career Training Center
1 Northeast 19th St.
Miami 33132
305-573-1600

James Lorenzo Walker Vocational-
Technical Center
3702 Estey Ave.
Naples 33940
941-495-7599

Haney Vocational-Technical Center
3016 Hwy. 77
Panama City 332405
904-769-2191 x139

St. Augustine Technical Center
298 Collins Ave.
St. Augustine 32084
904-829-1056

Pinnellas Technical Education Centers
St. Petersburg Campus
9091 34th St. S.
St. Petersburg 33711
813-895-3671 x201

ITT Technical Institute
4809 Memorial Hwy.
Tampa 33634
813-885-23244

Tampa Technical Institute
2410 East Busch Blvd.
Tampa 33612
813-935-5700

United Electronics Institute
3924 Coconut Palm Dr.
Tampa 33619
813-626-2999

Winter Park Tech
901 Webster Ave.
Winter Park 32789
407-647-6366

GEORGIA

Atlanta Area Technical Institute
1560 Stewart Ave.
Atlanta 30310
404-756-3700

DeVry Institute of Technology
250 N. Arcadia Ave.
Atlanta 30030
404-292-7900

Massey College of Business and
Technology
Lenox Center, 3355 Lenox Rd.
Atlanta 30326
404-816-4533

Augusta Technical Institute
3116 Deans Bridge Rd.
Augusta 30906
404-796-6900

Carroll County Area Vocational-Technical
School
997 South Hwy. 16
Carrollton 30116
404-836-6800

Professional Career Development
Institute
3597 Parkway Ln., Suite 100
Norcross 30092
404-729-8400

Coosa Valley Technical Institute
785 Cedar Ave.
Rome 30161
706-295-6206

Okefenokee Technical Institute
1701 Carswell Ave.
Waycross 31501
912-287-6584; 800-255-0056

IDAHO

Eastern Idaho Technical College
1600 South 2500 E.
Idaho Falls 83404
208-524-3000; 800-662-0261

ILLINOIS

Computer Learning Center of Chicago
200 S. Michigan
Chicago 60604
312-427-2700; 800-252-3393

DeVry Institute of Technology
3300 N. Campbell
Chicago 60618
773-929-8500

ITT Technical Institute
375 W. Higgins Rd.
Hoffman Estates 60195
708-519-9300

INDIANA

ITT Technical Institute
5115 Oak Grove Rd.
Evansville 47715-2340
812-479-1441

Indiana Vocational Technical College
Ivy Tech State College–Northeast
Gary 46409
219-981-1111

Ivy Tech State College–Central Indiana
P.O. Box 1763
Indianapolis 46202
317-921-4882

Ivy Tech State College–Wabash Valley
7999 U.S. Hwy. 41 S.
Terre Haute 47802
812-299-1121

Computer Technician Career Starter

KANSAS
Northwest Kansas Area Vocational-
Technical School
Box 668
Goodland 67735
913-899-3641

Kaw Area Technical School
5724 Huntoon
Topeka 66604
913-273-7140

KENTUCKY
Interactive Learning Systems
6612 Dixie Hwy., Suite 2
Florence 41042
606-282-8989

Computer Education Services
981 South 3rd St.
Louisville 40203
502-583-2860

Louisville Technical Institute
3901 Atkinson Dr.
Louisville 40218
502-456-6509; 800-844-6528

Institute of Electronic Technology
509 South 30th St.
Paducah 42001
502-444-9696; 800-995-4438

LOUISIANA
Louisiana State University
143 Pleasant Hall
Baton Rouge 70803-1520
504-388-6325; FAX: 504-388-3691

Sullivan Technical Institute
1710 Sullivan Dr.
Bogalusa 70427
504-732-6640

Southwest Louisiana Technical Institute
P.O. Box 820
Crowley 70527-0820
318-788-7521

Louisiana Technical College–Sowella
Campus
3820 Bennett Johnston Ave.
Lake Charles 70615
318-491-2688; 800-256-0483

Tulane University College
Microcomputer
200 Broadway, Suite 218
New Orleans 70118
504-866-0131; FAX: 504-861-4261

Ayers Institute
2924 Knight St., Suite 318
Shreveport 71105
318-868-3000

Shreveport Bossier Vocational-Technical
Institute
P.O. Box 78527
Shreveport 71137
318-676-7811

MARYLAND
Arundel Institute of Technology
1808 Edison Hwy.
Baltimore 21213
301-327-6640

RETS Technical Training Center
1520 South Caton Ave.
Baltimore 21227
410-644-6400

TESST Electronics and Computer
Institute
5122 Baltimore Ave.
Hyattsville 20781
301-864-5750

48

CDI Career Development Institute
10461 Mill Run Circle, Suite 120
Owings Mills 21117
410-356-1600

Computer Institute
611 Rockville Pike, Suite 5
Rockville 20852
301-424-8443

MASSACHUSETTS
Franklin Institute of Boston
41 Berkley St.
Boston 02116
617-423-4630

Bristol Community College
777 Elsbree St., D-103
Fall River 02720-7395
508-678-2811-2531;
FAX: 508-678-2876

Wentworth Technical School
191 Spring St.
Lexington 02173
508-371-9977; 800-292-3228

Computer Learning Center
5 Middlesex Ave.
Somerville 02145
617-776-3500; 800-698-3535

Computer-Ed Business Institute
100 Commerce Way
Woburn 01801
617-933-7681

MICHIGAN
SER Business and Technical Institute
9301 Michigan Ave.
Detroit 48210
313-846-2240

Ross Technical Institute
20820 Greenfield Rd., 1st Fl.
Oak Park 48237
313-967-3100

High-Tech Learning
7531 East Eight Mile Rd.
Warren 48091
810-758-6060

MINNESOTA
Anoka-Hennepin Technical College
1355 West Hwy. 10
Anoka 55303
612-576-4796; FAX: 612-576-4802

North Hennepin College
Center for Training and Development
7411 85th Ave. N.
Brooklyn Park 55445
612-424-0880; FAX: 612-424-0889

Dunwoody Institute
818 Dunwoody Blvd.
Minneapolis 55403-1192
612-374-5800; 800-292-4625

Minneapolis Community and Technical
Institute
1501 Hennepin Ave. S.
Minneapolis 55403
612-341-7040

St. Cloud Technical College
Center for Inovation & Economic
Development
1540 Northway Dr.
St. Cloud 56303
320-202-6493; FAX: 320-654-5568

Saint Paul Technical College
235 Marshall Ave.
St. Paul 55102
612-221-1360; 800-227-6029

MISSISSIPPI
Choctaw County Vocational Center
Box 298
Ackerman 39735
601-285-3205

Leland Vocational-Technical Center
Southeast Deer Creek Dr. E.
Leland 38756
601-686-5025

MISSOURI
Cape Girardeau Area Vocational-
Technical School
301 N. Clark Ave.
Cape Girardeau 63701
314-334-0826

ITT Technical Institute
13505 Lakefront Dr.
Earthcity 63045
314-298-7800

DeVry Institute of Technology
11224 Holmes Rd.
Kansas City 64131
816-941-2810; 800-821-3109

Ranken Technical Institute
4431 Finney Ave.
St. Louis 63113
314-371-0233; FAX: 314-371-0241

MONTANA
May Technical College
1306 Central Ave.
Billings 59102
406-259-7000

Computer School
Upper Level, Reeder's Alley
Helena 59601
406-442-3366

Helena Vocational-Technical Center
1115 Roberts St.
Helena 59601
406-444-6800

NEBRASKA
ITT Technical Institute
9814 M St.
Omaha 68127-2056
402-331-2900

NEW HAMPSHIRE
New Hampshire Technical College
11 Institute Dr.
Concord 03301
603-271-6663; FAX: 603-271-6667

New Hampshire Technical Institute
Institute Dr., Box 2039
Concord 03302-2039
603-225-1863; 800-247-0179

NEW JERSEY
Metropolitan Technical Institute
11 Daniel Rd.
Fairfield 07006
201-227-8191

DeVry Institute of Technology
630 U.S. Hwy. 1
North Brunswick 08902-3362
800-333-3879

National Education Center–RETS
Campus
103 Park Ave.
Nutley 07110
201-661-0600

Computer Learning Center
160 E. Rte. 4
Paramus 07652
201-845-6868

Chubb Institute for Computer
Technology
8 Sylvan Way, P.O. Box 342
Parsippany 07054-0342
201-685-4976; 800-248-2237

Trenton Central Area Vocational-
Technical School
Greenwood Ave. & Chambers St.
Trenton 08609
609-989-2431

DeVry Technical Institute
479 Green St.
Woodbridge 07095
908-750-3399

NEW MEXICO
Albuquerque Career Institute
111 Wyoming NE
Albuquerque 87123
505-268-2000; 800-274-5627

NEW YORK
Rochester Business Institute
1 Lomb Memorial Dr.
Rochester 14623
716-475-6631

White Plains Adult Education Center
228 Fisher Ave.
White Plains 10606
914-422-2333

NORTH CAROLINA
ECPI Computer Institute
1121 Wood Ridge Center Dr.
Charlotte 28217
704-357-0077

ECPI College of Technology
7015 G. Albert Pick Rd.
Greensboro 27409-9654
910-665-1400

OHIO
Stark Technical College
6200 Frank Ave. NW
Canton 44720
216-494-6170

MTI Business College
1140 Euclid Ave.
Cleveland 44115
216-621-8228

DeVry Institute of Technology
1350 Alum Creek Dr.
Columbus 43209
614-253-7291

Technology Education Center
288 South Hamilton Rd.
Columbus 43213
614-759-7700; 800-383-3233

ITT Technical Institute
3325 Stop Eight Rd.
Dayton 45414-9915
513-454-2267

RETS Electronics School
116 Westpark Rd.
Dayton 45459
513-433-3410

Stautzenberger College
1637 Tiffin Ave.
Findlay 45840
419-423-2211; FAX: 419-423-0725

Stautzenberger College
5355 Southwyck
Toledo 43614
419-866-0261; FAX: 419-867-9821

OKLAHOMA
Northeast Oklahoma Area Vocational
Technical Center
Pryor Site, Box 825
Pryor 73095
918-825-5555

Mid America Vocational-Technical
School
Box H
Wayne 73095
405-449-3391

OREGON
Skilltronics Vocational Institute
9375 SW Commerce Circle
P.O. Box 755
Wilsonville 97070
503-682-3909

PENNSYLVANIA
Computer Learning Network
1110 Fernwood Ave.
Camp Hill 17011
717-761-1481; 800-338-8037

Tri-State Computer Institute
5757 W. 26th St.
Erie 16506
814-838-3596

Hiram G. Andrews Center
727 Goucher St.
Johnstown 15905
814-255-8200; 800-762-4211

Electronic Institutes
19 Jamesway Plaza
Middletown 17057-4851
717-944-2311; 800-884-2731

Computer Tech
107 Sixth St., Fulton Bldg.
Pittsburgh 15222
412-391-4197; 800-447-8324

Computer Learning Center
3600 Market St.
University City 19104-2684
215-222-6450; 800-252-3393

Advanced Career Training
69th and Market Sts., 2nd Fl.
McClatchy Bldg.
Upper Darby 19082
215-352-3600

Pennsylvania College of Technology
One College Ave.
Williamsport 17701
717-326-3761; 800-367-9222

SOUTH CAROLINA
Greenville Technical College
Dean of Enrollment Management
Box 5616
Greenville 29606-5616
803-250-8154; 800-723-0673

ITT Technical Institute
One Marcus Dr.
Greenville 29615
864-288-0777

SOUTH DAKOTA
Mitchell Technical Institute
821 N. Capital St.
Mitchell 57301-2062
605-995-3024; 800-952-0042

Southeast Technical Institute
2301 Career Pl.
Sioux Falls 57107-1302
605-336-7624; 800-247-0789

TENNESSEE
State Technical Institute at Memphis
5983 Macon Cove
Memphis 38134-7693
901-337-4180

ITT Technical Institute
441 Donelson Pike
Nashville 37214-8029
615-889-8700

Tennessee Technology Center
100 White Bridge Rd.
Nashville 37209
615-741-1241

TEXAS

ITT Technical Institute
2201 Arlington Downs Rd.
Arlington 76011
817-640-7100

Richland College
12800 Abrams Rd.
Dallas 75243-2199
972-238-6225; FAX: 972-238-6957

Microcomputer Technology Institute
17164 Blackhawk Blvd.
Friendwood 77546
713-996-8180; 800-445-9957

ITT Technical Institute
15621 Blue Ash Dr., Suite 160
Houston 77090-5818
713-873-0512; 800-879-6486

Microcomputer Technology Institute
7277 Regency Sq.
Houston 77036
713-974-7181; 800-344-1990

Texas State Technical College of Waco
3801 Campus Dr.
Waco 76705
817-867-4800; 800-867-8784

UTAH

Certified Careers Institute
2661 Washington Blvd., Rm. 203
Ogden 84401
801-621-4925

Certified Careers Institute
1455 West 2200 S., Suite 200
Salt Lake City 84119
801-973-7008

VIRGINIA

Computer Learning Center
6295 Edsall Rd., Suite 210
Alexandria 22312
703-823-0300

TESST Electronics Institute
1400 Duke St.
Alexandria 22314
703-548-4800; 800-488-3778

ATI Career Institute
7777 Leesburg Pike, Suite 100 S.
Falls Church 22043
703-821-8570

ECPI Computer Institute
1919 Commerce Dr., Suite 200
Hampton 23666
804-838-9191

Norfolk Technical-Vocational Center
1330 N. Military Hwy.
Norfolk 23502
757-441-5625

A.R. Burton Voc-Tech School
1760 Roanoke Blvd.
Salem 24153
540-857-5002

ECPI Computer Institute
4303 West Broad St.
Richmond 23230
804-359-3535

ECPI College of Technology
5555 Greenwich Rd.
Virginia Beach 23462
800-966-3274

WASHINGTON

Lake Washington Vocational-Technical
Institute
11605 132nd Ave. NE
Kirkland 98034
206-828-5505

ITT Technical Institute
12720 Gateway Dr., Suite 100
Seattle 98168-3333
206-244-3300

Interface Computer School
N. 4601 Monroe, 3rd Fl.
Spokane 99205
509-327-7717; 800-999-7717

WEST VIRGINIA
Carver Career and Technical Education
Center
4799 Midland Dr.
Charleston 25306
304-348-1965

Computer Tech
Country Club Rd. Ext.
Fairmont 26554
304-366-5100; 800-447-8324

WISCONSIN
Gateway Technical College–Elkhorn
Campus
East Centralia St.
Elkhorn 53121
414-741-6100

Southwest Wisconsin Technical College
1800 Bronson Blvd.
Fennimore 53809
608-822-3262; 800-362-3322

Moraine Park Technical College
235 N. National Ave.
Fond du Lac 54935
414-922-8611

Madison Area Technical College
3550 Anderson St.
Madison 53704
608-246-6676

MBTI Business Training Institute
606 W. Wisconsin Ave.
Milwaukee 53203
414-272-2192

DIRECTORY OF VENDOR-AFFILIATED COMPUTER TRAINING PROGRAMS

Training Programs Offering Both Microsoft And Novell Courses

Since training programs may update their course offerings frequently, call the schools you're interested in to get the latest information. When available for a particular school, toll-free numbers, fax numbers, and web addresses are provided in the list below. If separate phone numbers are not listed for Novell and Microsoft training, then the information for both programs should be available from the main phone number listed.

ALABAMA
ATHENA Computer Learning Center, Inc.
#1 Perimeter Park South, Suite 400
Birmingham, AL 35243
615-244-1681 (Novell)
205-967-6661 (Microsoft)

New Horizons Computer Learning
Center
One Office Park, Suite 305
Mobile, AL 36609
334-460-0690

ALASKA
MicroAge InfoSystems Services
510 W Tudor Rd., Suite 109
Anchorage, AK 99503
907-762-9107 (Novell)
907-562-4488 (Microsoft)

ARIZONA
IKON/MIDAK
2700 N Central Avenue, 9th Floor
Phoenix, AZ 85004
602-266-9029 (Novell)
602-266-8512 (Microsoft)

Micro Professionals, Inc.
6991 E Camelback Rd., Suite D-300
Scottsdale, AZ 85251
602-945-0992;
FAX: 602-994-3482

CBSI
5005 S Ash Avenue
Tempe, AZ 85282
602-820-7141;
FAX: 602-820-7275

New Horizons Computer Learning
Center
725 S. Rural Road, Suite C-207
Tempe, AZ 85281
602-736-9300

Training Solutions
2121 S 48th St., Suite 106
Tempe, AZ 85282
602-431-1100;
http://www.tsolutions.com

ARKANSAS
Microsolutions Inc.
East Joyce Boulevard, Suite 1
Fayetteville, AR 72703
501-973-4545;
http://www.microsolutions.net

Complete Computing Inc.
400 West 7th Street
Little Rock, AR 72201
501-372-3379;
800-880-2949;
http://www.complete.com

CALIFORNIA
HTR, Inc.
600 Corporate Point, Suite 320
Culver City, CA 90230
800-882-6420;
FAX: 310-645-7761

New Horizons Computer Learning
Center
100 Corporate Point, Suite 288
Culver City, CA 90230
310-348-1144;
FAX: 310-348-1970

Executrain of California
17877 Von Karman Ave., Suite 150
Irvine, CA 92714
800-300-6440;
FAX: 714-221-0333

Evernet Education Services, Inc.
5777 West Century Blvd., Suite 1610
Los Angeles, CA 90045
310-642-0222;
FAX: 310-642-4606

Infotec Commercial Systems
1990 South Bundy Dr,. Suite 540
Los Angeles, CA 90025
310-442-2204 (Microsoft)
714-755-7155 (Novell)
800-282-7999;
http://www.infotecweb.com

Westcon Services Corp
5161 Lankershim Blvd., Suite 120
North Hollywood, CA 91601
818-763-9711;
800-756-6640;
FAX: 818-763-9767

ComputerFOCUS
2901 Ventura Road, Suite 100
Oxnard, CA 93031
805-988-6600;
FAX: 805-988-6844

New Horizons Computer Learning
Center
1215 Howe Avenue
Sacramento, CA 95825
916-641-8500;
http://www.newhorizons.com

TeKnowlogy, Inc.
50 California St., Suite 1600
San Francisco, CA 94111
888-358-7246;
FAX: 415-394-8961

TeKnowlogy, Inc.
181 Metro Dr., Suite 279
San Jose, CA 95110
408-453-6300;
888-358-7246;
FAX: 408-453-6314

Infotec Commercial Systems
3100 S Harbor Blvd., Suite 100
Santa Ana, CA 92704
714-755-7120;
http://www.infotecweb.com

Infotec Commercial Systems
4677 Old Ironsides Drive, Suite 300
Santa Clara, CA 95054
408-654-9370;
FAX: 408-654-1313;
http://www.infotecweb.com

New Horizons Computer Learning
Center
2185 N California, Suite 300
Walnut Creek, CA 94596
510-933-9955
FAX: 510-932-6562

TeKnowlogy, Inc.
2999 Oak Rd., Suite 200
Walnut Creek, CA 94596
888-358-7246;
FAX: 510-939-2716

COLORADO
Knowledge Alliance, Inc.
12100 East Iliff Ave., Suite 100
Aurora, CO 80014
303-338-7100 (Novell)
303-338-7113 (Microsoft)
http://www.kalliance.com

Knowledge Alliance, Inc.
4949 Pearl E Circle, #101
Boulder, CO 80301
303-338-7118;
FAX: 303-938-9623

New Horizons Computer Learning
Center
1675 Broadway, Suite 1420
Denver, CO 80202
303-745-0100 (Novell)
303-745-2022 (Microsoft)
http://www.nhdenver.com

Productivity Point International
720 South Colorado Blvd., Suite 200
Denver, CO 80222
303-756-5756;
FAX: 303-758-4723

CCTI, Inc
5500 Greenwood Plaza Blvd., Suite 130
Englewood, CO 80111
303-741-2284;
FAX: 303-741-6814

CONNECTICUT
Nextage
401 Merritt 7
Norwalk, CT 06851
203-849-3388;
FAX: 203-849-3004

LEARNINGEXPRESS

20 Academy Street, P.O. Box 7100, Norwalk, CT 06852-9879

FREE! TEN TIPS TO PASSING ANY TEST

To provide you with the test prep and career information you need, we would appreciate your help. Please answer the following questions and return this postage paid survey. As our Thank You, we will send you our "Ten Tips To Passing Any Test" – surefire ways to score your best on classroom and/or job-related exams.

Name : _____

Address : _____

_____

Age : _____ Sex : ☐ Male ☐ Female

Highest Level of School Completed : ☐ High School ☐ College

1) I am currently :

　　A student — Year/level: _____

　　Employed — Job title: _____

　　Other — Please explain: _____

2) Jobs/careers of interest to me are :

　　1. _____

　　2. _____

　　3. _____

3) If you are a student, did your guidance/career counselor provide you with job information/materials? _____

　　Name & Location of School: _____

　　_____

　　_____

　　_____

4) What newspapers and/or magazines do you subscribe to or read regularly? _____

　　_____

5) Do you own a computer? _____

　　Do you have Internet access? _____

　　How often do you go on-line? _____

6) Have you purchased career-related materials from bookstores?

　　_____

　　If yes, list recent examples: _____

　　_____

7) Which radio stations do you listen to regularly (please give call letters and city name)?

　　_____

　　_____

8) How did you hear about this LearningExpress book?

　　An ad? _____

　　If so, where? _____

　　An order form in the back of another book? _____

　　A recommendation? _____

　　A bookstore? _____

　　Other? _____

9) Title of the book this card came from:

　　_____

LearningExpress books are also available in the test prep/study guide section of your local bookstore.

LEARNINGEXPRESS

The new leader in test preparation and career guidance!

LearningExpress is an affiliate of Random House, Inc.

Directory of Computer Training Programs

Connecticut Computer Service, Inc.
101 East Summer Street
Plantsville, CT 06479
860-276-1285;
FAX: 860-276-1289

DELAWARE
Online Consulting, Inc.
300 Delaware Avenue, 14th Floor
Wilmington, DE 19801
302-658-3018-22
800-288-8221
FAX: 302-658-4051

DISTRICT OF COLUMBIA
Catapult
1717 K Street NW., Suite 407
Washington, DC 20006
703-758-1860;
FAX: 202-296-6773

Future Enterprises, Inc.
1331 Pennsylvania Ave. NW., Suite 1301
Washington, DC 20004
202-662-7610;
202-662-7676;
FAX: 202-662-7606

FLORIDA
Tech Data Education, Inc.
14450 46th Street North
Clearwater, FL 34622
800-834-8764;
FAX: 813-524-8750

Dershya Institute
5728 Major Blvd., Suite 307
Orlando, FL 32819
407-351-5052;
FAX: 407-354-5483

New Horizons Computer Learning
Center
31 West Garden St., Suite 200
Pensacola, FL 32501
904-434-3414
FAX: 904-433-9586

Systemark Of Orlando, Inc.
265 N Wymore Rd.
Winter Park, FL 32789
407-644-4779;
FAX: 407-644-3986

GEORGIA
HTR, Inc
The South Terraces, 115 Perimeter
Center Place, Suite 415
Atlanta, GA 30346
301-881-1010;
800-882-6420;
http://www.htr.com

New Horizons Computer Learning
Center
1706 N E Expressway
Atlanta, GA 30329
404-235-3500;
FAX: 404-235-3518

Tech Data Education, Inc.
400 Pinnacle Way, Suite 415
Norcross, GA 30071
800-834-8764;
FAX: 770-447-3735

HAWAII
Computer Training Academy/Network
Resources
550 Palea St., Suite 222
Honolulu, HI 96819
808-839-1200;
FAX: 808-839-4844

IDAHO
Computerland - The Learning Center
4795 Emerald, Suite A
Boise, ID 83706
208-345-8024;
FAX: 208-345-8011

ILLINOIS

New Horizons Computer Learning
Center
2 North Lasalle Mezzanine Level
Chicago, IL 60602
312-332-0419;
FAX: 312-332-5440

Productivity Point International
208 S Lasalle St., Suite 2010
Chicago, IL 60604
312-332-3865;
FAX: 630-920-2143

TeKnowlogy, Inc.
311 South Wacker Dr., Suite 200
Chicago, IL 60606
312-332-3665;
888-358-7246 ;
FAX: 312-693-9985

TeKnowlogy, Inc.
8420 W Bryn Mawr Ave., Suite 520
Chicago, IL 60631
312-332-3865;
888-358-7246;
FAX: 773-693-9985

Levi, Ray, & Shoup, Inc.
2401 W Monroe St.
Springfield, IL 62704
217-793-3800;
FAX: 217-698-0858

INDIANA

KSM Consulting, LLC
11711 North Meridian, Suite 780
Carmel, IN 46032
317-580-8407;
FAX: 317-580-8449

New Horizons Computer Learning
Center
11611 N Meridian St., Suite 200
Carmel, IN 46032
317-575-7600
FAX: 317-575-7640

Automated Office Solutions, Inc.
401 East Indiana
Evansville, IN 47711
812-428-7068;
FAX: 812-428-7126;
http://www.aos-evv.com

IOWA

XLConnect
940 Golden Valley Drive
Bettendorf, IA 52722
319-344-3112 (Novell)
319-344-3120 (Microsoft)
http://www.xlconnect.com

Help Desk
4110 NW 114th St.
Des Moines, IA 50322
515-276-1770;
FAX: 515-276-2077

KANSAS

Network Knowledge, Inc.
7844 Quivira Road
Lenexa, KS 66216
913-962-5267;
FAX: 913-962-0455
http://www.netknow.com

IKON Office Solutions-Technology
Service
7950 College Blvd
Overland Park, KS 66210
913-451-0033-375 (Novell)
451-003-3913 (Microsoft)
http://www.ikon-kc.com

New Horizons Computer Learning
Center
3985 E Harry
Wichita, KS 67218
316-687-2600;
FAX: 316-687-3850

KENTUCKY
Infotec Commercial Systems
2020 Liberty Road Suite 110
Lexington, KY 40505
606-367-2000 (Novell)
606-367-2002 (Microsoft)
http://www.ameridata.com/adl/

Micro Computer Solutions, Inc.
1601 Alliant Ave
Louisville, KY 40299
502-261-0000
FAX: 502-261-0001

XLConnect
9410 Bunsen Way, Suite 150
Louisville, KY 40220
502-493-1629 (Novell)
502-495-2500 (Microsoft)
FAX: 502-493-1646
http://www.xlconnect.com

LOUISIANA
New Horizons Computer Learning
Center
3925 N I-10 Service Rd., Suite 117
Metairie, LA 70002
504-456-3600 (Novell)
504-456-3605 (Microsoft)
FAX: 504-456-0225
http://newhorizons-no.com

New Horizons Computer Learning
Center
2924 Knight Street, Suite 380
Shreveport, LA 71105
318-869-1256 (Novell)
318-869-4999 (Microsoft)
FAX: 318-869-4915

MARYLAND
IKON Office Solutions-Technology
Service
10420 Little Patuxent Parkway
Columbia, MD 21044
410-715-5100
FAX: 703-893-9858

HTR, Inc.
6110 Executive Blvd Suite 810
Rockville, MD 20852
800-882-6420
FAX: 301-881-6577

MASSACHUSETTS
Boston University Corp. Education
Center
12 Post Office Square
Boston, MA 02109
800-BU-TRAIN
FAX: 508-649-2162

New Horizons Computer Learning
Center
99 Summer Street, Suite 310
Boston, MA 02110
617-229-9565
FAX: 617-229-9552

New Horizons Computer Learning
Center
5 Old Concord Road
Burlington, MA 01803
617-229-9565
http://www.nhboston.com

Productivity Point International/Boston
155 Federal St., Suite 901
Boston, MA 02110
617-928-1912-1218 (Novell)
617-964-5858 (Microsoft)
http://www.ppi-boston.com

New Horizons Computer Learning
Center
5 Old Concord Road
Burlington, MA 01803
617-229-9565
FAX: 617-229-9552

Productivity Point International/Boston
Three Newton Executive Park, Suite 102
Newton Lower Falls, MA 02162
617-928-1912
FAX: 617-964-5263

Pinnacle Education Center
92 Montvale Avenue, Suite 4400
Stoneham, MA 02180
617-279-4005
FAX: 617-279-4009

Boston University Corp. Education
Center
72 Tyng Road
Tyngsboro, MA 01879
800-BU-TRAIN
FAX: 508-649-6926

Tech Data Education, Inc.
60 Hickory Drive
Waltham, MA 02154
813-539-7429
FAX: 617-890-5192

MICHIGAN
National Tech Team, Inc.
835 Mason, Suite 200
Dearborn, MI 48124
313-277-2277
FAX: 313-277-5833

Productivity Point International
3769 Three Mile Road NW
Grand Rapids, MI 49544
616-735-1000
FAX: 616-791-4355

IKON Office Solutions-Technology
Service
5700 Crooks Rd., Suite 450
Troy, MI 48098
248-879-8800
FAX: 248-879-1070

MINNESOTA
Agiliti, Inc Norwest Financial Center
7900 Xerxes Ave South
Bloomington, MN 55431
612-820-9661
FAX: 612-820-9601

ExecuTrain
8500 Normandale Lake Blvd., Suite 110
Bloomington, MN 55437
612-921-8844 (Novell)
612-921-8913 (Microsoft)

Benchmark Computer Learning, Inc.
4510 West 77th St #210, Suite 300
Edina, MN 55435
612-896-6800 (Novell)
612-896-6840 (Microsoft)
http://www.benchmarklearning. com

MISSOURI
New Horizons Computer Learning
Center
2326 Millpark Dr.
St Louis, MO 63043
314-429-3311
FAX: 314-429-3790

NEBRASKA
New Horizons Computer Learning
Center
4827 Pioneers Blvd.
Lincoln, NE 68506
402-489-8811 (Novell)
402-331-4123 (Microsoft)
http://www.asiweb.com/nh

Knowledge Alliance, Inc.
1010 N 96th St., Suite 101
Omaha, NE 68114
402-391-4888
FAX: 402-391-4844

NEVADA
Learning Center, Inc.
2972 Meade Avenue
Las Vegas, NV 89102
702-365-8885;
FAX: 702-365-8148

Productivity Point International
2580 Sorrel St.
Las Vegas, NV 89102
702-365-1900
FAX: 702-365-1910

Productivity Point International-Reno
5301 Longley Lane, Bldg. A #7
Reno, NV 89511
702-829-8300
FAX: 702-829-8307

NEW HAMPSHIRE
New Horizons Computer Learning
Center
460 Amherst Street
Nashua, NH 03063
603-882-4900
FAX: 603-882-3267

Micro C Training Center
195 Commerce Way, Suite I
Portsmouth, NH 03801
TEL: 603-436-7324
FAX: 603-430-7854

NEW JERSEY
AlphaNet Learning Centers/AlphaNet
Solutions, Inc.
7 Ridgedale Ave.
Cedar Knolls, NJ 07927
201-539-9800 (Novell);
201-267-0088 (Microsoft)

Infotec Commercial Systems
100 Menlo Park Drive, Suite 317
Edison, NJ 08837
908-205-0198; 908-205-1979;
http://www.infotecweb.com

AlphaNet Learning Centers
33 Wood Avenue South
Iselin, NJ 08830
908-632-2999; FAX: 201-539-4707

Infotec Commercial
18000 Horizon Way, Suite 700
Mt. Laurel, NJ 08054
609-231-1717

Track On Technical Education Centers
140 E Ridgewood Ave Mack Center III
Paramus, NJ 07652
201-986-0900 (Novell);
201-634-4007 (Microsoft)

NEW MEXICO
Data Management Systems, Ltd.
6755 Academy Rd. NE, Suite A
Albuquerque, NM 87109
505-821-1150; FAX: 505-821-1113

NEW YORK
Westcon Services Corp
450 Sawmill River Rd., Bldg. # 3
Ardsley, NY 10502
800-LAN-TEACH; FAX: 914-674-6910

IKON Office Solutions-Technology
Service
2295 Millersport Hwy.
Getzville, NY 14068
716-688-5353; FAX: 716-688-5355

IKON Office Solutions-Technology
Service
1174 Troy Schenectady Road
Latham, NY 12110
518-786-3666; FAX: 518-786-0906

Infotec Commercial Systems
One World Trade Center, Suite 2167
New York, NY 10048
212-524-0234
http://www.infotecweb.com

Netlan Technology Center
29 West 38th St., 17th Fl.
New York, NY 10018
212-768-2273; FAX: 212-768-3498

New Horizons Computer Learning
Center
One Penn Plaza, Suite 5000, 50th Fl.
New York, NY 10119-0002
212-273-7420 (Novell);
212-273-7436 (Microsoft);
http://www.newhorizons.com

IKON Office Solutions-Technology
Service
1200 C Scottsville Rd.
Rochester, NY 14624
716-436-8180; FAX: 716-436-1816

Westcon Services Corp
6900 Jericho Turnpike, Suite 312
Syosset, NY 11791
800-LAN-TEACH; FAX: 516-496-4335

NORTH CAROLINA
IKON Office Solutions-Technology
Service
412 East Blvd.
Charlotte, NC 28203
704-339-0023
FAX: 704-339-0970

New Horizons Computer Learning
Center
9144 Arrowpoint Blvd., Suite 110
Charlotte, NC 28273
704-522-9747
FAX: 704-522-9752

Alphanumeric Systems, Inc.
3801 Wake Forest Road
Raleigh, NC 27690
919-781-7575
FAX: 919-781-7517
http://www.alphanumeric.com

OHIO
New Horizons Computer Learning
Center
10653 Techwoods Circle
Blue Ash, OH 45242-2846
513-554-0111
http://www.newhorizons.com

Software School
4750 Wesley Ave., Suite M
Cincinnati, OH 45212
513-841-0444
FAX: 513-841-0446
http://www.softwareschool.com

Vanstar
4141 Rockside Road, Suite 210
Cleveland, OH 44131
216-642-8676
FAX: 216-642-8678

XLConnect Solutions, Inc
5350 Transportation Blvd., Suite 9
Cleveland, OH 44125
216-663-4430
FAX: 216-663-7725
http://www.xlconnect.com

Blue Chip Computers Company
1630 E Stroop Road
Dayton, OH 45429
937-299-4594
FAX: 937-298-5798
http://www.bluechip.com

Babbage-Simme
l5131 Post Road, Suite 100
Dublin, OH 43017-1367
614-764-8777
FAX: 614-764-9049

New Horizons Computer Learning
Center
6000 Rockside Woods Blvd., Suite 100
Independence, OH 44131
216-520-0066
FAX: 216-520-0060

OKLAHOMA

Network Enterprise Technologies, Inc.
2448 East 81st St Suite 299
Tulsa, OK 74137
918-496-2244
FAX: 918-492-1840

New Horizons Computer Learning
Center
4943 S 78th E Avenue
Tulsa, OK 74145
918-664-4400
FAX: 918-664-4468

PENNSYLVANIA

Infotec Commercial Systems
Iron Run Corporate Center
7540 Windsor Drive, Suite 40
Allentown, PA 18195
888-234-8890
http://www.infotecweb.com

Catapult
300 Berwyn Park Dr., Suite 111
Berwyn, PA 19312
610-725-1945
800-244-3382
FAX: 610-695-8849

IKON Office Solutions
Naamans Career Center
7 Creek Parkway
Boothwyn, PA 19061
610-494-9000
FAX: 610-494-2090

eLearn It, Corp
1325 Morris Drive, 3rd Floor
Chesterbrook, PA 19087-5594
610-408-9858
FAX: 610-408-9888

Infotec Commercial Systems
1250 Virginia Dr., Suite 160
Fort Washington, PA 19034
215-619-9030
FAX: 215-619-9022

Inacom Information Systems
1850 William Penn Way, Suite 205
Lancaster, PA 17601
717-397-7766
FAX: 717-293-1870
http://www.iis-centpa.com

Infotec Commercial Systems
Greenfield Corporate Center
1817 Olde Homestead Lane, Suite 206
Lancaster, PA 17601
888-234-8890
http://www.infotecweb.com

Online Consulting, Inc.
15th & Ranstead, Suite 1800
Philadelphia, PA 19102
302-658-3018
FAX: 302-658-4051

Riverhead Training, Inc.
355 Fifth Ave., Suite 902
Pittsburgh, PA 15222
412-391-7473 (Novell)
412-261-6755 (Microsoft)

SOUTH CAROLINA

IKON Office Solutions-Technology
Service
11 Technology Circle
Columbia, SC 29203
FAX: 803-935-1111

IKON Office Solutions-Technology
Service
535 N Pleasantburg Dr., Suite 210
Greenville, SC 29607
864-421-0011
FAX: 864-421-0012

SOUTH DAKOTA

Training Partners, LLC
2701 S Minnesota Ave., Suite 3
Sioux Falls, SD 57105
605-339-3221 (Novell)
605-361-6076 (Microsoft)
http://training.iw.net

TENNESSEE
Computer Learning Center
10368 Wallace Alley St., Suite 9
Kingsport, TN 37663
800-898-5151
FAX: 423-279-1280

Computer Learning Center
9111 Cross Park Dr Bldg C, Suite 100
Knoxville, TN 37923
423-691-1515
FAX: 423-691-4265

ATHENA Computer Learning Center, Inc
6401 Poplar Ave., Suite 120
Memphis, TN 38119
615-244-1681 (Novell)
901-685-7046 (Microsoft)
http://www.athenaclc.com

New Horizons Computer Learning
Center
227 French Landing Dr., Suite 400
Nashville, TN 37228
615-251-6955
FAX: 615-251-6925

TEXAS
Infotec Commercial Systems
9420 Research Bldg. 3, Suite 200
Austin, TX 78759
800-880-0029

Productivity Point International
7800 Shoal Creek, Suite 100-E
Austin, TX 78757
512-452-1200
FAX: 512-459-9565

CompUSA, Inc
1445 Ross Ave., Suite 4550
Dallas, TX 75202
214-969-5955
FAX: 214-969-5920

New Horizons Computer Learning
Center
5151 Belt Line Road #550
Dallas, TX 75240
972-490-5151
FAX: 972-490-8251

Productivity Point International
2711 LBJ Freeway, Suite 900
Dallas, TX 75234
972-484-1000
FAX: 972-484-0058

TeKnowlogy, Inc
1950 Stemmons Freeway, Suite 2048
Dallas, TX 75207
214-746-5267
888-358-7246
FAX: 214-746-5589

Computer Technology Associates
1515 Cessna, Suite 100
El Paso, TX 79925
915-771-7115
FAX: 915-771-7572

Avatar Computer Solutions, Inc
256 N Sam Houston Parkway E
Suite 268
Houston, TX 77060
281-999-1300
888-503-0503
FAX: 281-999-7070

Infotec Commercial Systems
2700 Post Oak Blvd., Suite 1150
Houston, TX 77056
713-552-9415

TeKnowlogy, Inc
3555 Timmons Ln., Suite 900
Houston, TX 77027
214-373-5214
888-358-7246
FAX: 713-961-1430

Tech Data Education, Inc.
6230 N Beltline Rd. Suite 301
Irving, TX 75063
800-834-8764
FAX: 214-756-0628

Productivity Point International
45 N.E. Loop 410 Center Plaza Bldg,
Suite 300
San Antonio, TX 78216
210-342-6500
FAX: 210-340-5177

UTAH
GSE Erudite Software, Inc.
2494 North University Ave
Provo, UT 84604
801-576-8800
FAX: 801-576-8815

New Horizons Computer Learning
Center
332 W Bugatti
Salt Lake City, UT 84115
801-485-6200
http://www.slcnewhorizons.com

GSE Erudite Software, Inc
406 W 10600 S
South Jordan, UT 84095
801-576-8800
FAX: 801-576-8815

VERMONT
SymQuest Group, Inc
50 Cherry St
Burlington, VT 05401
802-658-9838
FAX: 802-658-9843
http://www.symquest.com

VIRGINIA
Computer Education Services, Inc.
1755 Jefferson Davis Hwy
Crystal Square 5, Ste 1101
Arlington, VA 22202
703-415-1645
FAX: 703-415-2583

Framatome Technologies,
Information Svcs.
1300 Old Graves Mill Rd
Lynchburg, VA 24502
804-832-3810 (Novell)
804-832-3803 (Microsoft)

IKON Office Solutions-Technology
Service
1430 Springhill Rd., Suite 600
McLean, VA 22102-3000
703-893-3382
FAX: 703-893-9858

Electronic Systems
11832 Rock Landing Drive, Suite 100
Newport News, VA 23606
757-873-1045 (Novell)
757-877-4440 (Microsoft)
http://www.esi.com

Infotec Commercial Systems
999 Waterside Dr., Suite 400
Norfolk, VA 23510
757-446-0800
FAX: 757-446-0810
http://www.infotecweb.com

Catapult
12020 Sunrise Valley Dr., Suite 230
Reston, VA 22091
703-758-1860
FAX: 703-758-1854

Orange Technologies, Inc
6564 Loisdale Court, Suite 110
Springfield, VA 22150
301-840-5927
FAX: 703-924-8977

Electronic Systems
361 Southport Circle
Virginia Beach, VA 23452
757-497-8000
FAX: 757-497-2095

WASHINGTON
Knowledge Alliance, Inc.
3290 146th Place S.E. Bldg A
Bellevue, WA 98007
206-401-6264 (Novell);
425-957-9500 (Microsoft);
http://www.kalliance.com

MicroAge InfoSystems Services
606 120th Ave. NE, Suite D102/103
Bellevue, WA 98005
206-637-1056; 800-816-4276;
FAX: 425-637-1079

Infotec Commercial Systems
One Union Square
600 University, Suite 320
Seattle, WA 98101
800-684-4080;
http://www.infotecweb.com

USConnect Seattle
Two Union Square
601 Union St., Suite 2700
Seattle, WA 98101-2392
206-224-7690 (Novell);
206-224-7687 (Microsoft);
FAX: 206-622-8658

New Horizons Computer Learning Center
1322 N Post St.
Spokane, WA 99201-2520
509-328-8077; FAX: 509-328-7603

WISCONSIN
Executrain of Milwaukee
18650 W. Corporate Drive, Suite 115
Brookfield, WI 53045
414-792-1880; FAX: 414-792-1881

New Horizons Computer Learning Center
5315 Wall St., Suite 140
Madison, WI 53704
608-246-8000; FAX: 608-245-5001

Training Programs Offering Microsoft Courses

Since training programs update their course offerings frequently, it's best to call the programs you're interested in to get the latest information. Some of these schools may offer more than Microsoft training. Web addresses are provided when available.

ALABAMA
Executrain of Birmingham
4601 Southlake Pkwy., Suite 100
Birmingham 35244-1015
205-987-9877;
http://www.executrain.com

Executrain of Huntsville
1525 Perimeter Pkwy., Suite 270
Huntsville 35806
205-987-9877

Intergraph Corporation/Hunstville
One Madison Industrial Park
Huntsville 35894
205-730-6700; 800-240-3000;
http://www.intergraph.com/cust

MBS, Inc.
4920-C Corporate Dr.
Huntsville 35805-6204
205-837-2620; http://www.mbsinc.com

Executrain of Montgomery
4001 Carmichael Center, Suite 215
Montgomery 36106
205-987-9877;
http://www.executrain.com

ALASKA
Compueaze, Inc.
1577 C St., Suite 205
Anchorage 99501
907-272-2888; http://www.nbsys.com

ARIZONA
Training Associates, Inc.
1201 S. Alma School Rd., Suite 4250
Mesa 85210
602-649-2711;
http://www.trainingassociates.com

CTS Southwest
777 E. Missouri Ave.
Phoenix 85014
602-274-1600;
http://www.infinisys.com

Executrain of Phoenix, Inc.
2800 North 44th St., Suite 650
Phoenix 85008
602-955-7787; http://www.etphx.com

GSE Erudite Software, Inc.
3111 N. Central Ave., Suite 100
Phoenix 85012
602-279-7100; 800-378-3483;
http://www.erudite.com

Productivity Point International
2020 N. Central Ave., Suite 690
Phoenix 85004
602-252-1984;
http://www.propoint.com

ARKANSAS
Connally Systems
10025 W. Markham, Suite 240
Little Rock 72205
501-225-8868;
http://www.connally.com

CALIFORNIA
New Horizons Computer Learning
Center
303 N. Glenoaks Blvd., Suite L100
Burbank 91502
714-431-9229;
http://www.newhorizons.com

Of the Inland Empire
1090 East Washington St., Suite H
Colton 92324
909-426-4900; http://newhorizons.com

American Digital Technologies
3100 Bristol St., Suite 380
Costa Mesa 92626-3051
714-433-1300; http://www.adttsa.com

Unitek Consulting Corp
39465 Paseo Padre Pkwy. # 2900
Fremont 94538
510-249-1060; http://www.unitek.com

Ascolta Training Co., Llc.
2351 McGaw Ave.
Irvine 92688
714-477-2000;
http://www.ascoltatraining.com

Creative Business Concepts, Inc.
One Technology Dr., Bldg. H
Irvine 92618
714-727-3104;
http://www.cbconcepts.com

Quickstart Technologies
1500 Quail St., 6th Fl.
Newport Beach 92660
800-326-1044;
http://www.quickstart.com

IS Inc.
1320 National Drive
Sacramento 95834
916-928-1700; http://www.isinc.com

Ascolta Training Co., Llc.
11777 Sorrento Valley Rd.
San Diego 92121
619-794-3074;
http://www.ascoltatraining.com

Executrain of San Diego
10180 Fraternal Court, 3rd Fl.
San Diego 92121
619-550-4746;
http://home.connectnet.com/etsd

Quickstart Technologies
4510 Executive Dr., Suite P2
San Diego 92121
800-826-1044;
http://www.quickstart.com

Productivity Point International
562 Mission St., Suite 400
San Francisco 94105-2915
415-243-0100;
http://www.propoint.com

Computer Solutions
3150 Almaden Expwy., Suite 214
San Jose 95118
408-629-4845; http://www.drael.com

Ikon/Datawiz
1500 Fashion Island Blvd., Suite 209
San Mateo 94404
415-571-1300;
http://www.datawiz.com

Knowledge Alliance Inc.
5 Hutton Centre Dr., Suite 210
Santa Ana 92707-5754
714-427-0305

Productivity Point International
4699 Old Ironsides Dr., Suite 270
Santa Clara 95054-1824
408-748-2990;
http://www.propoint.com

Quickstart Technologies
5201 Great America Pkwy., Suite 332
Santa Clara 95054
800-326-1044;
http://www.quickstart.com

COLORADO

Aris/Softeach Corporation
1355 So. Colorado Blvd., Suite 606
Denver 80222
303-759-1127; http://www.aris.com

Berger & Co.
1350 17th St., Suite 300
Denver 80202
303-571-4557; http://www.berger.com

Executrain of Denver
Panorama Corporate Center
7630 S. Chester St., Suite 160
Englewood 80112
303-436-1000

The Parsec Group, Inc.
405 Urban St., Suite 212
Lakewood 80228
303-763-9600; http://www.parsec.com

Uci Software Consulting & Training
12596 West Bayaud Ave., Suite 330
Lakewood 80228
800-732-0333

CONNECTICUT

Desai Systems, Inc.
44-2 Griffin Rd. S.
Bloomfield 06002-1352
860-286-9696; http://www.desai.com

HBM Technology Group
17 Britton Dr.
Bloomfield 06002-3616
860-243-1000; http://www.hbm.com

Command Systems, Inc.
76 Batterson Park Rd.
Farmington 06032
860-409-2000;
http://www.commandsys.com

CPCE, Inc.–Glastonbury
95 Glastonbury Blvd., 4th Fl.
Glastonbury 06033
203-925-0400; http://www.cpce.com

CPCE, Inc. –Shelton
2 Corporate Dr., Suite 310
Shelton 06484
203-925-0400

DISTRICT OF COLUMBIA
HTR, Inc. –Washington
1150 18th St. NW, Suite 765
Washington 20036
301-881-1010; http://www.htr.com

ICI Systems, Inc.
1730 K St. NW, Suite 915
Washington 20006
202-887-0510; http://www.icisys.com

Knowledge Alliance
5335 Wisconsin Ave. NW, Suite 809
Washington 20015
202-686-4133;
http://www.kalliance.com

Knowlogy Corporation
818 Connecticut Ave. NW, 4th Fl.
Washington 20006
703-532-1000;
http://www.knowlogy.com

FLORIDA
Homnick Systems, Inc.
2300 Glades Rd., Suite 150 Tower West
Boca Raton 33431
561-368-0010;
http://www.homnick.com

Executrain of Fort Lauderdale
6365 NW 6th Way, Suite 205
Fort Lauderdale 33309-6130
305-470-2001;
http://www.executrain.com

Consultech, Inc.
100 Wharfside Way
Jacksonville 32207
904-399-3555;
http://users.ilnk.com/consultech

The Network Group, Inc.
104 S. Harbor City Blvd.
Melbourne 32901
407-723-8550; http://www/tng.net

Ace Education, Inc.
16698 NW 54th Ave.
Miami 33014
305-622-3334;
http://www.acetrain.com

Executrain of Miami
8240 NW 52nd Terrace, Suite 500
Miami 33166-7765
305-470-2001;
http://www.miami.executrain.com

Merisel Latin America, Inc.
1629 NW 84th Ave.
Miami 33126
305-908-7191; http://www.chsla.com

Service Pointe
450 E. South St., Suite 204
Orlando 32801
407-422-4999

Techknowquest
7536 Municipal Dr.
Orlando 32819
407-248-0400; http://www.tkq.com

Powercerv Technologies Corporation
400 North Ashley Dr., Suite 2700
Tampa 33602
813-226-2600;
http://www.powercerv.com

GEORGIA

Executrain of Atlanta
1000 Abernathy Rd., Suite 400
Atlanta 30328-5614
770-396-9200

Ikon-Valinor, Inc.
One Concourse Pkwy., Suite 770
Atlanta 30328-5564
800-370-8258; http://www.valinor.com

Intellinet Corporation
3475 Lenox Rd., Suite 700
One Live Oak Center
Atlanta 30326
404-233-7700

Kaplan Communications
1950 Century Blvd., Suite 4
Atlanta 30345
404-633-8535;
http://www.kapcom.com

Omni Technology Centers
47 Perimeter Center East, Suite 400
Atlanta 30346
770-395-0055;
http://www.omnitechnology.com

Productivity Point International
3490 Piedmont Rd. NE, Suite 520
One Securities Center
Atlanta 30305-4808
770-816-5833;
http://www.propoint.com

GE Capital IT Solutions–Norcross
5550 Peachtree Pkwy., Suite 500
Norcross 30092-2533
770-447-3362

Intergraph Corporatioin
3300 Highlands Pkwy., Suite 260
Smyrna 30082
800-240-3000;
http:www.intergraph.com/cust

HAWAII

Information Systems Technology Center
Bldg. 221, Box 140
Pearl Harbor 96860-5200
808-474-4918;
http://www.intecph.navy.mil

ILLINOIS

Intergraph Corporation
85 W. Algonquin, Suite 600
Arlington Heights 60005
800-240-3000;
http:www.intergraph.com/cust

Database Designs, Inc.
1645 N. Barclay Blvd.
Buffalo Grove 60089-4544
847-634-9355; http://www.dbdinc.com

Wordlink, Inc.–Champaign
2009 Fox Dr.
Champaign 61820-7300
217-359-9378;
http://www.wordlink.com

Checkpoint
120 North Lasalle St., Suite 1030
Chicago 60602
630-279-9030;
http://www.sark.com/checkpoint.html

Information Management Group
One IBM Plaza, Suite 2000
Chicago 60611
312-222-9400;
http://www.imginfo.com

Metamor Technologies, Ltd.
1 N. Franklin, Suite 1500
Chicago 60606
312-251-4280;
http://www.metamor.com

Software Spectrum TSG
8755 West Higgins Rd., Suite 400
Chicago 60631
800-624-2033;
http://www.swspectrum.com

Productivity Point International
1419 Lake Cook Rd., Suite 390
Deerfield 60015-5230
847-940-8495;
http://www.propoint.com

Wordlink, Inc.–East Moline
1201 Seventh St.
East Moline 61244
217-359-9378;
http://www.wordlink.com

Knowledge Alliance, Inc.
2611 Corporate West Dr.
Lisle 60532-3600
630-505-2150;
http://www.schulco.com

Productivity Point International
1250 E. Diehl Rd., Suite 302
Naperville 60563
630-920-7190;
http://www.propoint.com

Teknowlogy Education Centers
1717 Naper Blvd., Suite 301
Naperville 60563-8827
888-358-7246;
http://www.teknowlogy.com

Productivity Point International
3601 Algonquin Rd., Suite 601
Rolling Meadows 60008
847-670-8490;
http://www.propoint.com

Wordlink, Inc.–Schaumburg
1920 N. Thoreau Dr., Suite 121
Schaumburg 60173-4151
847-397-5004;
http://www.wordlink.com

INDIANA
Integrated Information Services
11911 N. Meridian St.
Carmel 46032
317-581-7600

Network Services Group, Inc.
8275 Allison Pointe Trail, Suite 130
Indianapolis 46250
317-579-5806;
http://www.networkservicesgroup.com

Newmedia, Inc.
200 S. Meridian St., Suite 220
Indianapolis 46225-1076
317-638-7900

Productivity Point International
10585 N. Meridian St., Suite 300
Indianapolis 46290
317-573-2320;
http://www.propoint.com

Computerland of Northern Indiana
3371 Cleveland Rd., Suite 202
South Bend 46628
219-273-2012; http://clni.com

Computrain Learning Center, Inc.
400 Wabash Ave., Suite B-10
Terre Haute 47807
812-235-7419;
http://www.computrain.indiana.net

IOWA
Erb's Business Machines, Inc.
645 32nd Ave. SW
Cedar Rapids 52404
319-364-5159

Productivity Point International
805 Wright Brothers Blvd.
Cedar Rapids 52404
319-398-7099;
http://www.propoint.com

KANSAS
Executrain of Kansas City
6900 College Blvd., Suite 670
Overland Park 66211-1536
913-451-2898

Productivity Point International–Kansas
City
10100 87th St., Suite 107
Overland Park 66212-4628
913-383-3400;
http://www.propoint.com

Solutech, Inc.
7300 College Blvd., Suite 165
Lighton Plaza I
Overland Park 66210
800-676-9393;
http://www.solutechinc.com

Executrain of Wichita
727 North Waco, Suite 180
Wichita 67203-3951
316-267-4000;
http://www.executrain.com/wichita

KENTUCKY
Goodwell, Inc.
10001 Linn Station Rd., Suite 105
Louisville 40223
502-426-8519;
http://www.newhorizons.com

Kizan Technologies, Inc.
200 Whittington Pkwy., Suite 101
Louisville 40222-4900
502-327-0333; http://www.kizan.com

Solutech, Inc.
Hurstbourne Place
9300 Shelbyville Rd., Suite 703
Louisville 40222
800-676-9393;
http://www.solutechinc.com

A Technological Advantage, Inc.
500 W. Jefferson St., Suite 1440
Citizens Plaza
Louisville 40202
502-583-3224; http://www.atai.com

LOUISIANA
Productivity Point International
5536 Superior Dr., Suite A
Baton Rouge 70816-6064
504-295-4130;
http://www.propoint.com

Executrain of New Orleans
1450 Poydras St., Suite 610
New Orleans 70112-6010
504-593-2200;
http://www.executrain.com

Productivity Point International
1515 Poydras Ave., Suite 1380
New Orleans 70112-3723
504-523-5111;
http://www.propoint.com

MAINE
Productivity Point International
Stroudwater Estate
10 Harry Harmon Dr.
Portland 04102-1954
207-772-2335;
http://www.propoint.com

MARYLAND
HTR Inc.
100 E. Pratt St., Suite 1530
Baltimore 21202-1009
301-881-1010; http://www.htr.com

New Horizons CLC
7125 Ambassador Rd., Suite 100
Baltimore 21244-2733
410-597-9722;
http://www.newhorizons.com

Technologies Inc.
4800 Hampden Lane
Bethesda 20814
301-657-6281; http://www.feddata.com

Global Knowledge Network–Baltimore
140 Lakefront Dr.
Cockeysville 21030
919-469-7051;
http://www.globalknowledge.com

System Source
338 Clubhouse Rd.
Hunt Valley 21031
410-771-5544; http://www.syssrc.com

Global Knowledge
Network–Washington
8201 Corporate Dr., Suite 900
Landover 20785-2237
919-469-7051;
http://www.globalknowledge.com

Computer Technology Services, Inc.
1700 Rockville Pike, Suite 260
Rockville 20852
301-468-9377;
http://www.computer-classes.com

MASSACHUSETTS
Glow Training Center
40 Nagog Park, 3rd Fl.
Acton 01720
508-264-0222;
http://www.ultranetcom/~gtc

Compuworks Systems, Inc.
330 Congress St.
Boston 02210-1216
617-944-4751;
http://www.compuworks.com

UCI Software Consulting & Training, Inc.
92 Montvale Ave., Suite 3950
Stoneham 02180
800-884-1772; http://www.ucicorp.com

SAIC Synetics System Operation
540 Edgewater Dr.
Wakefield 01880
617-245-1312;
http://www.synetics.saic.com

HTR, Inc.–Waltham
230 Third St., 5th Fl.
Waltham 02154
800-882-6420; http://www.htr.com

Vanstar Corporation –Waltham
9 Hillside Ave., 5th Fl.
Waltham 02154
617-890-0009; http://www.vanstar.com

Data General Corporation–Open
Systems Training
4400 Computer Dr.
Educational Services Mail Stop G-153
Westboro 01580
800-633-8649

New Horizons CLC of Boston
2000 West Park Dr.
Westboro 01581
617-229-9565;
http://www.nhboston.com

Technology Training Group
10 State St., 1st Fl.
Woburn 01801
888-342-5884; http://www.ttgtrain.com

MICHIGAN
Productivity Point International
1350 Highland Dr., Suite F
Ann Arbor 48104
419-891-9151;
http://www.propoint.com

American Systems Technology, Inc.
888 W. Big Beaver Rd., Suite 420
Troy 48084-1526
248-362-4100; http://amsystech.com

Pathway Systems
1607 E. Big Beaver Rd., Suite 350
Troy 48083
248-740-7654;
http://www.pathsys.com

Productivity Point International–Troy
5600 New King St., Suite 365
Troy 48098
248-952-5212;
http://www.propoint.com

MINNESOTA
Total Solutions Group
3601 Minnesota Dr., Suite 520
Bloomington 55435
612-831-8320; http://www.tsg-usa.com

Valley Micro Associates, Inc.
2051 Killebrew Dr., Suite 415
Bloomington 55425
612-858-1127;
http://www.valleymicro.com

Bridge Data
601 Carlson Pkwy., Suite 360
Minnetonka 55305
612-933-3336;
http://www.bridgedata.com

Response, Inc.
416 South Broadway
Rochester 55904
507-252-4790

MISSISSIPPI
Athena
805 South Wheatley St., Suite 550
Ridgeland 39157
601-957-3944;
http://www.athenaclc.com

MISSOURI
Solutech, Inc.
117 South Main St., Suite 300
St. Charles 63301
800-676-9393;
http://www.solutechinc.com

Daugherty Systems
One City Place Dr., Suite 240
Saint Louis 63141-7066
314-432-8200;
http://www.daugherty.com

Productivity Point International
8961 Page Blvd., Suite A
Saint Louis 63114-6120
314-426-2200

Systems Service Enterprises, Inc.
795 Office Pkwy., Suite 101
St. Louis 63141-7166
314-997-4700

A Technological Advantage, Inc.
12400 Olive Blvd.
Suite 425, Paragon Bldg
St. Louis 63141
314-576-3696

Wordlink Inc. –St. Louis
12647 Olive Blvd., Suite 100
St. Louis 63141-6345
314-878-1422;
http://www.wordlink.com

NEBRASKA
Executrain of Omaha
7171 Mercy Rd., Suite 550
Omaha 68106-2620
402-397-7772

Inacom Information Systems–Omaha
9300 Underwood Ave., Suite 170
Omaha 68114-2685
402-392-3990;
http://www.inacom.com

Solutech, Inc.
13220 Birch Dr.
Omaha State Bank Bldg., Suite 220
Omaha 68164
402-491-3007

NEW HAMPSHIRE
Productivity Point International
Independence Pl., 15 Constitution Dr.
Bedford 03038
603-471-0848;
http://www.propoint.com

Ikon-Valinor, Inc.–New Hampshire
7 Perimeter Rd.
Manchester 03103-3343
800-370-8258; http://www.valinor.com

E/TAC, Inc.
98 Spit Brook Rd., Suite 401
Nashua 03062
603-891-0995; http://www.etac.com

NEW JERSEY
CALC–Canterbury
100 Hanover Ave.
Cedar Knolls 07927
201-898-6227;
http://www.canterburyxcel.com

New Horizons CLC
111 Wood Ave. S.
Iselin 08830
908-767-1000;
http://www.newhorizons.com

Emtec Inc.
817 East Gate Dr.
Mt. Laurel 08054
609-235-2121; http://www.emtc.com

Chubb Corporate Training
10 Sylvan Way
Parsippany 07054-3825
201-971-3072;
http://www.chubb-csvcs.com

Delta Corporate Services
129 Littleton Rd.
Parsippany 07054
973-334-6260;
http://www.deltacorp.com/esg

Alpha Technologies, Inc.
88 Centennial Ave.
Piscataway 08854
732-980-1800;
http://www.alpha88.com

Integrated Computer Management
5 Becker Farm Rd., 280 Corporate Center
Roseland 07068
201-535-3400;
http://www.icmsolutions.com

Alphanet Solutions, Inc.
Park 80 West, 3rd Fl.
GS Pkwy. at Rte. 80
Saddle Brook 07663
201-539-9800

New Horizons Computer Learning Center
1044 Laurel Oak Rd., Suite 5
Voorhees 08043-3512
609-435-4080;
http://www.nhphilly.com

NEW MEXICO
Kemtah Group
6605 Uptown Blvd. NE, Suite 370
Albuquerque 87110-4200
505-883-5959;
http://www.kemtah.com

NEW YORK
Dgs Enterprises Unlimited, Inc.
4 Pine West Plaza
Albany 12205-5515
518-869-1305

Briarcliffe College
1055 Stewart Ave.
Bethpage 11714
516-470-6000; http://www.bcl.org

Productivity Point International
One Huntington Quadrangle,
Suite 3N02
Melville 11747-4401
516-694-0202;
http://www.propoint.com

Pride Technologies, Inc.
290 Broadhollow Rd.
Melville 11747
800-9PRIDE9

CALC–Canterbury
780 Third Ave., Concourse Level
New York 10017-2024
201-898-6227;
http://www.canterburyxcel.com

CGI Systems, Inc.
500 Fifth Ave., 32nd Fl.
New York 10110
610-725-1945

Computrainers Corp.
48 East 43rd St.
New York 10017
212-573-8383;
http://www.computrainers.com

Datacom Technology Group, Inc.
350 Fifth Ave., Suite 3805
New York 10118
212-629-5720;
http://www.datacom1.com

Executrain of New York City
489 Fifth Ave., 2nd Fl.
New York 10017
212-338-0967

Global Knowledge Network–New York
One Liberty Plaza
165 Broadway, 27th Fl.
New York 10006-1404
919-469-7051;
http://www.globalknowledge.com

Ikon-Valinor, Inc. –New York
125 Maiden Ln., 2nd Fl.
New York 10038
800-370-8258; http://www.valinor.com

Objectarts
195 Broadway, Suite 1801
New York 10007
212-566-4223;
http://www.objectarts.com

Productivity Point International
19 W. 44th St., 17th Fl.
New York 10036-5902
212-398-6410;
http://www.propoint.com

Vanstar Corporation–New York
5 Penn Plaza, 17th Fl.
New York 10001
800-313-9549

Technology Training Solutions
28 Terminal Dr. S.
Plainview 11803
516-349-8877

Productivity Point International
100 Kings Park South, Suite 2700
Rochester 14617
716-467-0760;
http://www.propoint.com

NORTH CAROLINA

Atlas Online University, Inc.
224 Timberhill Place
Chapel Hill 27514
919-933-9798; http://www.atlasu.com

Productivity Point International
7031 Albert Pick Rd., Suite 302
Greensboro 27409
910-664-0380;
http://www.propoint.com

Computer Decisions, Inc.
2950 Gateway Centre Blvd.
Morrisville 27560
919-460-0071; http://www.cditrain.com

NORTH DAKOTA

Ekman Inc.
1700 42nd St., SW
Fargo 58103
701-281-5333;
http://www.corptechnologies.com

OHIO

Blue Chip Computers Company
4250 Creek Rd.
Cincinnati 45241
937-299-4594

Information Systems Research, Inc.
2 Crowne Point Ct., Suite 260
Cincinnati 45240
513-772-4636;
http://www.isresearch.com

Kizan Technologies, Inc.
Corporate Woods, 14500 Lake Forest
Drive
Cincinnati 45242
513-563-6000; http://www.kizan.com

Productivity Point International
11499 Chester Rd., Suite 2500
Cincinnati 45246-4012
513-772-5277;
http://www.propoint.com

Sarcom–Cincinnati
525 Vine St., Suite 400
Cincinnati 45202
513-421-0332; http://www.sarcom.com

Decarlo, Paternite, and Associates, Inc.
6155 Rockside Rd., Suite 110
Cleveland 44131-2220
216-524-2121; http://www.dpai.com

Vanstar Corporation–Columbus
500 W. Wilson Bridge Rd., Suite 130
Columbus 43085
614-841-7400

Xlconnect Systems, Inc.
1105 Schrock Rd., Suite 105
Columbus 43229
614-781-9500;
http://www.xlconnect.com

Productivity Point International
425 Metro Place North, Suite 200
Dublin 43017
614-793-4157;
http://www.propoint.com

Productivity Point International
1789 Indianwood Circle, Suite 140
Maumee 43537-4022
419-891-9151;
http://www.propoint.com

OKLAHOMA

Executrain of Oklahoma City
3817 NW Expwy., Suite 100
Oklahoma City 73112-1465
405-942-4494; http://www.etokc.com

Productivity Point International
210 Park Ave., Suite 2260
Oklahoma City 73102
405-235-8128;
http://www.propoint.com

Precision Computer Services, Inc.
11022 E. 51st St.
Tulsa 74146
918-663-2911; http://www.pcsi.net

OREGON
Aris Corporation
15201 NW Greenbrier Pkwy., Suite A-1
Beaverton 97006
503-645-2200; http://www.aris.com

Sequent Computer Systems, Inc.
15450 SW Koll Pkwy.
Beaverton 97006-6024
503-578-3040;
http://www.sequent.com/training

United Data Processing, Inc.
1600 NW Compton Dr., Suite 140
Beaverton 97006
503-690-6877; http://www.udp.com

Margre, Inc.
9400 SW Barnes Rd., Suite 100
Portland 97225
503-292-8900

Step Technology, Inc.
11130 SW Barbur Blvd.
Portland 97219
503-293-6377;
http://www.steptech.com

PENNSYLVANIA
Productivity Point International
1605 N. Cedar Crest Blvd., Suite 402
Allentown 18106
610-776-6114;
http://www.pctraining.com

Berkeley Corporation
2 Bala Plaza, Suite 504
Bala Cynwyd 19004
610-664-3880

Knowledge Alliance, Inc.
3 Valley Square, Suite 390
Blue Bell 19422
215-283-6000;
http://www.kalliance.com

Productivity Point
International–Harrisburg
4242 Carlisle Pike, Suite 151
Camp Hill 17011
610-776-6114;
http://www.pctraining.com

Maxwell Training Centers, Inc.
2860 Dekalb Pike
Norristown 19401
610-292-0450;
http://www.maxwelltrain.com

Global Knowledge Network–Pittsburgh
2016 Lebanon Rd., Suite 3
West Mifflan 15122
919-469-7051;
http://www.globalknowledge.com

Productivity Point International–Wilkes
Barre–Scranton
Garden Village Professional Center
16 Luzerne Ave., Suite 160
West Pittston 18643
610-776-6114;
http://www.pctraining.com

SOUTH CAROLINA
New Horizons CLC of Greenville
33 Villa Rd., Suite B-100
Greenville 29615
864-232-5828

TENNESSEE
Solutech, Inc.
1801 West End Ave.
Nashville 37203
314-947-9393;
http://www.solutechinc.com

TEXAS

Executrain of Austin
8310 Capitol of Texas Hwy., Suite 375
Austin 78731-1016
512-346-0101;
http://www.executrain.com/austin

Businessware Learning Centers, Inc.
4710 Bellaire Blvd., Suite 310
Bellaire 77401
713-665-1985; http://www.blcinc.com

Absolute!, Inc.
1950 Stemmons Frwy., Suite 5046
Dallas 75207-3109
214-746-5611;
http://www.absolute-edu.com

B. R. Blackmarr and Associates
1950 Stemmons Frwy., Suite 3031
Dallas 75207
214-744-4004

Berger & Company
2828 Routh St., Suite 350, Lock Box 17
Dallas 75201
214-922-8010; http://www.berger.com

Executrain of Dallas
12201 Merit Dr., Suite 350
Dallas 75251-2221
972-387-1212;
http://www.executrain/dal.com

Intergraph Corporation
8111 LBJ Frwy., Suite 1400
Dallas 75251
800-240-3000;
http:www.intergraph.com/cust

Knowledgepool, Inc.
5429 LBJ Frwy.
Dallas 75240
888-215-3872;
http://www.knowledgepool.com

Newdata Strategies
16415 Addison Rd., Suite 500
Dallas 75248
972-735-0001;
http://www.newdat.com

Software Spectrum Inc./TSG–Dallas
5001 Spring Valley Rd., Suite 920e
Dallas 75244
800-624-2033

Berger & Company
5 Greenway Plaza, Suite 1700
Houston 77046
713-627-7878; http://www.berger.com

Hilton Computer Strategies
6001 Savoy, Suite 207
Houston 77036-3322
713-782-6665; http://www.hcsnet.com

Newdata Strategies
1700 West Loop S., Suite 900
Houston 77027
713-626-5899;
http://www.newdat.com

Omni Technology Center of Houston, Llc.
15311 Vantage Pkwy. W., Suite 240
Houston 77032
713-981-3810;
http://www.omnitechnology.com

Productivity Point International
910 Travis St., Suite 2000
Houston 77002
713-650-0100;
http://www.propoint.com

Southern Methodist University
6575 West Loop S., Suite 700
Houston 77401
713-662-9768;
http://www.seas.smu.edu/netech/

UTAH
Executrain of Salt Lake City
7090 South Union Park Ave., Suite 550
Midvale 84047-4162
801-561-8511

Advanced Technical Center
3995 South 700 E., Tower III, Plaza
Level
Salt Lake City 84107
801-281-8448; http://www.atc-inc.com

GSE Erudite Software, Inc.
102 West 500 S., Suite 600
Salt Lake City 84115
801-533-0100; http://www.erudite.com

VIRGINIA
Ikon Office Solutions
1755 Jefferson Davis Hwy., Suite 800
Arlington 22202
703-883-0616; http://www.ikon.com

Republic Research Training Center, Inc.
1100 Wilson Blvd., Suite 810
Arlington 22209
800-476-4454; http://www.rrtc.com

Aris Corporation
3040 Williams Dr., Suite 100
Fairfax 22031-4618
703-641-1547; http://www.aris.com

Knowlogy Corporation
105 West Broad St., 5th Fl.
Falls Church 22046
703-532-1000;
http://www.knowlogy.com

HTR Inc.–Mclean
2000 Corporate Ridge Rd., Suite 700
Mclean 22102
301-881-1010; http://www.htr.com

IPC Technologies, Inc.
7200 Glen Forest Dr.
Richmond 23229
804-285-9300;
http://www.ipctech.com

Productivity Point International
10800 Midlothian Tpke.
Suite 126, Koger Center S.
Richmond 23235-4700
804-794-1145;
http://www.propoint.com

Republic Research Training Center, Inc.
7275 Glen Forest Dr., Suite 208
Richmond 23226
800-476-4454; http://www.rrtc.com

Gestalt Systems, Inc.
2070 Chain Bridge Rd., Suite G-40
Vienna 22182
703-748-1817;
http://www.gestalt-sys.com

Professional Software Engineering, Inc.
200 Golden Oak Court, Reflections II,
Suite 100
Virginia Beach 23452-6700
757-431-2400;
http://www.prosoft-eng.com

WASHINGTON
Aris Corporation
1750 112th Ave. NE Suite B-101
Bellevue 98004
425-462-4348

Executrain of Bellevue
10900 NE 8th St., Suite 1200
Bellevue 98004-4405
206-454-0844;
http://www.executrain.com

New Horizons Computer Learning
Center
1715 114th Ave. SE, Suite 120
Bellevue 98004-6906
425-454-4285;
http://www.newhorizons.com

Productivity Point International/Seattle
600-108th Ave. NE, Suite 847
Bellevue 98004
425-646-1830;
http://www.propoint.com

Olsy North America
22425 E. Appleway
Liberty Lake 99019-9534
509-927-4046;
http://www.hk.olivetti.com

Productivity Point International
606 W. 3rd Ave.
Spokane 99204
509-455-5054;
http://www.propoint.com

WEST VIRGINIA
Technology Solutions
405 Capitol St., Upper Atrium
Charleston 25301
304-344-5395

WISCONSIN
PC Solutions, Inc.
13400 W. Bishops Ln., Suite 270
Brookfield 53005
414-938-2139

PC Experience Center, Inc.
842 S. Military Ave.
Green Bay 54304-2114
920-490-5900;
http://www.pcexperience.com

Executrain of Minneapolis, Inc.
4600 American Pkwy., Suite 102
Madison 53704
414-792-1880;
http://www.executrain.com

Valcom/More Than Computers, Inc.
2249 Pinehurst Dr.
Middleton 53562-2540
608-836-8180

New Horizons CLC of Milwaukee
2100 N. Mayfair, Suite 200
Wauwatosa 53226
414-607-5600;
http://www.nhmilw.com

Training Programs Offering Novell Courses

Since training programs often change and update their course offerings, call the programs you're interested in to get the latest information. Some of these schools may offer more than Novell training.

ALABAMA
New Horizons Computer Learning
Center
601 Beacon Parkway West, Suite 106
Birmingham 35209
205-942-2522; 205-942-2540

New Horizons Computer Learning
Center
4960 Corporate Dr., Suite 150
Huntsville 35805
205-722-0211; FAX: 205-722-7926

ALASKA
Network Business Systems
1577 C St., Suite 205
Anchorage 99501
907-272-2888; FAX: 907-272-7117

ARIZONA
MicroAge InfoSystems Services
2828 N. 44th St., Suite A-100
Phoenix 85008
602-224-5500; FAX: 602-224-5501

New Horizons Computer Learning
Center
3600 E. University Dr., Suite B-1300
Phoenix 85034
602-437-3000 x133;
FAX: 602-437-1492

MindWorks Professional Education
Group
1525 N. Hayden Rd., Suite 57
Scottsdale 85257
602-874-1500; FAX: 602-990-0081

Training Solutions
2121 S. 48th St., Suite 106
Tempe 85282-1015
602-431-1100; FAX: 602-438-1161

DRA Software Training
3434 E. 22nd St., Suite 100
Tucson 85713
520-323-3434; FAX: 520-323-3411

New Horizons Computer Learning
Center
6377 E. Tanque Verde Rd., #200
Tucson 85715
520-290-5600

University of Arizona Extended
University
888 N. Euclid Ave., P.O. Box 210158
Tucson 85721-0158
520-626-5091; FAX: 520-621-3269

CALIFORNIA
Learning Tree University
20960 Knapp St.
Chatsworth 91311
818-882-5599; FAX: 818-882-1719

New Horizons Computer Learning
Center
1090 E. Washington St., Suite D-H
Colton 92324
909-426-4900 x137;
FAX: 909-426-4909

New Horizons Computer Learning
Center
3337 Michelson Dr., Concourse Level,
Suite 1
Irvine 92715
714-431-9218; FAX: 714-436-6382

CompUSA, Inc.
2049 Century Park East, Suite 810
Los Angeles 90067
310-552-2025; FAX: 310-552-3707

Executrain of California
865 S. Figueroa St., Suite 1150
Los Angeles 90017
800-300-6440; FAX: 213-488-7779

Martinez Adult School
l600 F St.
Martinez 94553-3298
510-228-3631; FAX: 510-228-1366

Innovative Solutions
475 14th St., Suite 450
Oakland 94612
510-433-1210; FAX: 916-928-9309

Infotec Commercial Systems
5776 Stoneridge Mall Rd., Suite 125
Pleasanton 94588
800-933-6685; FAX: 510-460-0824

Woodbridge & Associates
9513 Business Center Dr.
Rancho Cucamonga 91730-4500
909-989-8001; FAX: 909-986-8866

Computer Utilization, Inc.
3077 Fite Circle, Suite 6
Sacramento 95827
916-364-0203; FAX: 916-363-0476

Infotec Commercial Systems
8950 Cal Center Dr., Bldg. 3, Suite 135
Sacramento 95826
916-361-6920; FAX: 916-361-6931

Innovative Solutions
1320 National Dr.
Sacramento 95834
916-928-1700; FAX: 916-928-9309

Inacom Information Systems
11777 Sorrento Valley Rd.
San Diego 92121
619-794-3074; FAX: 619-481-9323

Vortex Data Systems
7480 Mission Valley Rd., Suite 100
San Diego 92108
619-497-6400 x274; FAX: 619-497-6410

Evernet Education Services, Inc.
71 Stevenson St., Suite 2120
San Francisco 94105
415-764-1400; FAX: 310-642-4606

Infotec Commercial Systems
455 Market St., Suite 1650
San Francisco 94105
408-654-9370; FAX: 415-786-5932

New Horizons Computer Learning
Center
One Embarcadero, Suite 200
San Francisco 94111
415-421-5151; FAX: 415-421-5518

New Horizons Computer Learning
Center
1231 E. Dyer Rd., Suite 140
Santa Ana 92705-5605
714-431-9218; FAX: 714-556-4612

Tech Data Education, Inc.
3621 S. Harbor Blvd., Suite 225
Santa Ana 92704
800-834-8764; FAX: 714-825-0951

Tech Data Education, Inc.
3350 Scott Blvd., Bldg. 39
Santa Clara 95054
813-539-7429; FAX: 408-567-1190

New Horizons Computer Learning
Center
4643 Quail Lakes Dr.
Stockton 95207
209-951-8500; FAX: 209-951-8799

LAN Specialists, Inc.
4030 Spencer St., Suite 107
Torrance 90503
310-214-1066; FAX: 310-542-2305

NovaQuest InfoSystems
19950 Mariner Ave.
Torrance 90503
310-793-4438; FAX: 310-370-9629

New Horizons Computer Learning
Center
920 Hampshire Rd., Suite S
Westlake Village 91361
805-777-4837; FAX: 805-496-9780

COLORADO

CCTI, Inc.
1065 Garden of the Gods Rd.,
Suite 105
Colorado Springs 80907
719-599-3790; FAX: 303-741-6814

New Horizons Computer Learning
Center
730 Citadel Dr. East, Suite 300
Colorado Springs 80909
719-380-0300; FAX: 719-380-8494

Applied Computer Technology
1221 W. Elizabeth
Ft Collins 80525
970-490-1849; FAX: 970-490-1439

CONNECTICUT

IKON Office Solutions–Technology
Service
One Barnard Ln.
Bloomfield 06002
860-243-1000 x184;
FAX: 860-769-5111

Connecticut Computer Service, Inc.
344 W. Main St.
Milford 06460
203-874-4546; FAX: 203-876-1106

New Horizons Computer Learning
Center
839 Marshall Phelps Rd.
Windsor 06095
860-298-7070; FAX: 860-298-7081

FLORIDA

Dataflex Corporation
861 Hercules Ave. N.
Clearwater 34625
813-562-2524; FAX: 813-562-2244

New Horizons Computer Learning
Center
311 Park Place Blvd., Suite 220
Clearwater 34619
813-791-6224; FAX: 813-791-4965

Productivity Point International
1260 N. University Dr., Suite 100
Fort Lauderdale 33322
954-723-9801; FAX: 954-723-9740

IKON Office Solutions–Technology
NW 35th Terrace
Fort Lauderdale 33309
800-925-3321; FAX: 954-484-0811

Productivity Point International
7020 AC Skinner Pkwy., Suite 180
Jacksonville 32256
904-281-9880; 904-281-9535

Dataflex Corporation
2300 Maitland Center Pkwy., Suite 122
Maitland 32751
800-989-5500 x2524; FAX:
407-660-2779

Knowledge Alliance
8600 NW 53 Terrace, Suite 200
Miami 33166
305-477-6755; FAX: 305-477-6753

Magic Box, Inc.
16698 NW 54th Ave.
Miami 33014
305-620-2770; FAX: 305-620-2737

Merisel Latin America, Inc.
1629 NW 84th Ave.
Miami 33122
305-718-2590; FAX: 305-718-2599

TrainX
14411 Commerce Way, Suite 400
Miami Lakes 33016
305-822-8010; FAX: 305-822-8033

Knowledge Alliance
1995 E. Oakland Park Blvd.
Oakland 33306
954-964-5496; FAX: 954-963-6753

Edutech
300 NW 82 Ave., #403
Plantation 33324
954-916-8528; FAX: 954-916-9110

Dataflex Corporation
500 A Capital Dr. SE, Suite 1
Tallahassee 32301
904-942-5400 x200; FAX:
904-878-5710

Productivity Point International
1497 Market St.
Tallahassee 32312

IKON Office Solutions–Technology
Service
5412-A Pioneer Park Blvd.
Tampa 33634
800-925-3321; FAX: 813-289-8088

Knowledge Alliance
2701 N. Rocky Point Dr., Suite 100
Tampa 33607
813-282-0380; FAX: 813-286-7704

Network Training Solutions, Inc.
5820 W. Cypress St., Suite H
Tampa 33607
813-287-8876; FAX: 813-289-3284

GEORGIA
Advanced Technology Group, Inc.
5600 Roswell Rd., Suite 120 N
Atlanta 30342
404-252-9611; FAX: 404-252-8118

Keeping Track Corporation
1718 Peachtree St., NW
Atlanta 30309-2409
404-815-1800; FAX: 404-815-0156

RGI Education Center
6020 Dawson Blvd., Suite I
Norcross 30093
770-409-3200 x118; FAX: 770-300-0076

HAWAII
Computer Training Academy/Network
Resources
Alii Place
1099 Alakea St., Suite 2112
Honolulu 96813
808-839-1200; FAX: 808-839-4844

Computer Training Company, Inc.
1001 Bishop Pacific Tower, Suite 1185
Honolulu 96813
808-522-8822; FAX: 808-522-8828

ILLINOIS
ExecuTrain
230 W. Monroe, Suite 2620
Chicago 60606
312-422-1506; FAX: 312-422-9778

IKON Office Solutions–Technology
Service
333 W. Wacker Dr., Suite 400
Chicago 60606
312-857-1500; FAX: 312-857-1515

Sentinel Technologies, Inc.
2550 Warrenville Rd.
Downers Grove 60515
630-769-4343; FAX: 630-769-1399

IKON Office Solutions–Technology
Service
501 W. Lake St., Suite 108
Elmhurst 60126
630-993-5340; FAX: 630-834-3349

Xerox Corporation
4415 W. Harrison St., Suite 501
Hillside 60162
708-649-4701; FAX: 708-649-4714

Mi-Tech Enterprises, Inc.
17 W. 662 Butterfield Rd., Suite 207
Oakbrook Terrace 60181
630-932-4585; FAX: 630-932-7299

PC Resources, Inc.
1030 W. Higgins Rd., Suite 305
Park Ridge 60068
847-825-6915 x15; FAX: 847-825-6918

PCDC
1002 E. Algonquin Rd., Suite 107
Schaumburg 60173
847-925-1100; FAX: 847-925-1160

Tech Data Education, Inc.
2050 E. Algonquin Rd., Suite 622
Schaumburg 60173
800-834-8764; FAX: 847-397-5773

INDIANA
Micro Computer Solutions, Inc.
101 Plaza E. Blvd., Suite 107
Evansville 47715
812-479-8260; FAX: 812-479-6540

Pinnacle Computer Services, Inc.
640 S. Heron Ave.
Evansville 47714
812-476-6662; FAX: 812-474-2332

KnowledgeLink
10022 Lantern Rd., Suite 100
Fishers 46038
317-842-4777; FAX: 317-577-8977

IKON Office Solutions
1625 Magnavox Way
Fort Wayne 46804
219-436-0743; FAX: 219-436-2633

Lantech of America, Inc.
8902 Vincennes Circle
Indianapolis 46268-3036
800-616-6255; FAX: 317-872-9944

XLConnect Solutions, Inc.
9455 Delegates Row
Indianapolis 46240
800-875-3669; FAX: 317-844-4128

IKON Office Solutions
3371 Cleveland Rd., Suite 202
South Bend 46628
219-273-2012; FAX: 219-273-2028

IOWA
Lantech of America, Inc.
2117 State St., Suite 150
Bettendorf 52722
319-355-2130; FAX: 319-355-2215

Iowa Electronics
260 33rd Ave. SW, Suite B
Cedar Rapids 52404
319-362-2448; FAX: 319-362-2735

New Horizons Computer Learning
Center
1850 Boyson Rd.
Hiawatha 52233
319-294-9035; FAX: 319-395-6096

KANSAS
New Horizons Computer Learning
Center
6405 Metcalf Ave., Bldg. 3
Overland Park 66202
913-677-9933; FAX: 913-677-4047

KENTUCKY
Pomeroy Computer Resources
1050 Elijah Creek Rd., Greater
Cincinnati Bench
Hebron 41048
606-586-1515 x4208;
FAX: 606-586-1494

Micro Computer Solutions, Inc.
771 Corporate Dr.
Lexington 40503
606-224-2345; FAX: 606-224-7008

Pomeroy Computer Resources
908 Dupont Rd.
Louisville 40207
502-893-2800 x177;
FAX: 502-893-0747

MAINE
Connecting Point
295 Forest Ave., 2nd Fl.
Portland 04104
207-772-1156; FAX: 207-879-7286

Valcom
50 Foden Rd.
South Portland 04106
207-775-5055; FAX: 207-775-0241

MARYLAND
Orange Technologies, Inc.
11C Firstfield Rd.
Gaithersburg 20878
301-840-1152; FAX: 301-840-2189

Global Knowledge Network
140 Lakefront Dr.
Hunt Valley 21030-2238
410-785-6300; FAX: 410-785-5321

MASSACHUSETTS
Boston University Corp. Education
Center
100 Cambridge Park Dr.
Cambridge 02140
800-BU-TRAIN; FAX: 508-649-2162

Boston University Corp. Education
Center
33 Commercial St.
Foxboro 02035
800-BU-TRAIN; FAX: 508-649-2162

MICHIGAN
New Horizons–CTSC
150 W. Jeffersen
Detroit 48226
313-525-1501 x1159;

FAX: 313-961-5626

New Horizons–CTSC
5800 Foremost Dr., Suite 100
Grand Rapids 49546
616-975-7500; FAX: 616-975-7501

SilverLake Resources
4024 Park East Court SE, Suite A
Grand Rapids 49546
616-956-6888; FAX: 616-957-4450

New Horizons–CTSC
14115 Farmington Rd.
Livonia 48154
313-525-1501 x1159;
FAX: 313-525-1401

PCDC
37450 Schoolcraft Rd., Suite 160
Livonia 48150
800-322-7232; FAX: 313-953-0656

Computer Data, Inc.
25786 Commerce Dr.
Madison Heights 48071
248-544-9900; FAX: 248-544-7155

Computer Data, Inc.
3899 Okemos Rd., Suite B
Okemos 48864
800-755-0142; FAX: 517-349-2169

Executrain of Detroit
25330 Telegraph Rd., Suite 210
Southfield 48034
810-352-9210; FAX: 810-352-9213

New Horizons–CTSC
100 Galleria Officentre, Suite 100
Southfield 48034
313-525-1501 x1159;
FAX: 248-204-1000

New Horizons–CTSC
340 E. Big Beaver
Troy Office Centre, Suite 100
Troy 48083
313-525-1501 x1159;
FAX: 248-824-1002

MISSISSIPPI
ATHENA Computer Learning Center, Inc.
Attium North
805 S. Wheatley St., Suite 550
Ridgeland 39157
615-244-1681; FAX: 601-957-2602

MISSOURI
Wordlink, Inc.
12647 Olive Blvd.
Creve Coeur 63141
314-878-1422; FAX: 314-878-2650

Computerland of Jefferson City
117 Commerce Dr.
Jefferson City 65110-5018
573-635-1607; FAX: 573-635-4227

NEBRASKA
HunTel
613 North 109th Plaza
Omaha 68154
402-492-2820; FAX: 402-492-2821

NEW HAMPSHIRE
Micro C Training Center
Hollis Village Marketplace, Bldg. 7
P.O. Box 1138
Hollis 03049
603-465-3110; FAX: 603-465-7903

NEW JERSEY
Brick Computer Associates & Computer
Science
515 Rte. 70
Brick 08723-4043
908-477-0975; FAX: 908-477-0962

Westcon Services Corporation
252 Fernwood Ave.
Edison 08837
800-LAN-TEACH; FAX: 212-225-1973

Tech Data Education, Inc.
16000 Horizon Way, Suite 600
Mt. Laurel 08054
800-834-8764; FAX: 609-423-7347

ICM Education Services
600 Alexander Rd., Bldg. 2, 2nd Fl.
Princeton 08540
800-426-9987; FAX: 201-535-8789

ICM Education Services
280 Corporate Center,
5 Becker Farm Rd.
Roseland 07068
201-535-3400; FAX: 201-535-8789

NEW MEXICO
New Horizons Computer Learning
Center
4665 Indian School Rd. NE, Suite 101
Albuquerque 87110
505-262-2222; FAX: 505-262-0222

NEW YORK
Command Services Corporation
1873 Western Ave.
Albany 12084
518-456-1000; FAX: 518-456-7878

Island Drafting & Technical Institute
128 Broadway
Amityville 11701
516-691-8733; FAX: 516-691-8738

ITS Education Center
55-2 Orville Dr.
Bohemia 11716
516-589-8666 x2081;
FAX: 516-563-4366

Aegis/Career Blazers Learning Center
445 Broadhollow Rd.
Melville 11747
516-756-2400; FAX: 516-756-2426

Aegis/Career Blazers Learning Center
290 Madison Ave., Suite 300
New York 10017
212-725-7900 x102; FAX: 212-725-8767

New Horizons Computer Learning
Center
40 Broad St.
New York 10004
212-971-7068; FAX: 212-239-9751

Westcon Services Corporation
Empire State Bldg.
350 Fifth Ave., Suite 6812
New York 10118
800-LAN-TEACH; FAX: 212-268-6890

Westcon Services Corporation
55 Broad St., 8th Fl.
New York 10004
800-LAN-TEACH; FAX: 212-809-0526

Logical Operations
500 Canal View Blvd.
Rochester 14623
716-240-7304; FAX: 716-240-7780

Command Services Corporation
1153 West Fayette St.
Syracuse 13204
315-472-9000; FAX: 315-472-9119

ICON
750 James St.
Syracuse 13203-2002
315-476-7981; FAX: 315-476-7984

IKON Office Solutions–Technology
Service
105 Twin Oaks Dr.
Syracuse 13204
315-433-8500; FAX: 315-433-9510

NORTH CAROLINA
Cedalion Education, Inc.
8401 University Executive Park Dr.,
Suite 100
Charlotte 28262
704-549-4765; FAX: 704-549-9680

Cedalion Education, Inc.
4020 Stirrup Creek Dr., Suite 109
Durham 27703
919-361-1944; FAX: 919-361-9537

Computer Education Services, Inc.
Headquarters Park, Beta Bldg. 2222
Chapel Hill Nelson Hwy., Suite 100
Durham 27713
919-544-3356; FAX: 919-544-3827

Cedalion Education, Inc.
7029 Albert Pick Rd.
Greensboro 27409
910-664-1127; FAX: 910-664-1184

NORTH DAKOTA
Ultra Connecting Point
303 S. Third St.
Bismarck 58504
701-258-6689; FAX: 701-258-0768

Corporate Technologies
1700 42nd St. SW
Fargo 58103
701-277-0011; FAX: 701-277-0012

OHIO
KnowledgeLink
525 Vine St., Suite 400
Cincinnati 45202
513-421-0332 x173; FAX: 513-421-2550

New Horizons Computer Learning
Center
10653 Techwoods Circle
Cincinnati 45242
513-554-0111 x2206;
FAX: 513-554-4050

PCDC
110 Boggs Ln., Suite 131
Cincinnati 45246
800-322-7232; FAX: 513-771-7729

XLConnect
2722 E. Kemper Rd.
Cincinnati 45241
513-672-8056; FAX: 513-672-8066

KnowledgeLink
8405 Pulsar Place
Columbus 43240
614-854-1369; FAX: 614-854-1090

XLConnect Solutions, Inc.
242 E. Campusview Blvd.
Columbus 43235
614-885-3645; FAX: 614-885-3057

New Horizons Computer Learning
Center
3136 Presidential Dr.
Fairborn 45324-2039
937-427-0111 x1115;
FAX: 937-427-4050

PCDC
401 Tomahawk Dr.
Maumee 43537
419-891-9700; FAX: 419-891-9702

McHale USConnect
31200 Bainbridge Rd.
Solon 44139
216-498-3550; FAX: 216-498-3623

KnowledgeLink
8555 Sweet Valley, Suite N
Valley View 44125
216-642-9850; FAX: 216-642-9855

Vanstar
500 W. Wilson Bridge, Suite 130
Worthington 43085
614-841-7400; FAX: 614-841-4599

OREGON
New Horizons Computer Learning
Center
8285 SW Nimbus Ave., Suite 170
Beaverton 97008-6401
503-641-8292; FAX: 503-641-1759

New Horizons Computer Learning
Center
c/o The Network Group
115 W. Eighth, Suite 120
Eugene 97401
503-641-8292; FAX: 503-641-1759

Micronet Systems, Inc.
1221 Disk Dr.
Medford 97501
541-858-9799;
FAX: 541-772-4225

Infotec Commercial Systems
Lincoln Tower
10260 SW Greenburg Rd., Suite 1000
Portland 97223
503-244-8900; FAX: 503-244-8300

MicroAge InfoSystems Services
9400 SW Barnes Rd., Suite 100
Portland 97225
800-496-4276; FAX: 503-292-7950

New Horizons Computer Learning
Center
East Village Park Business Center
3855 SW Wolverine, Bldg. A, Suite 2
Salem 97305
503-641-8292; FAX: 503-315-2223

PENNSYLVANIA
Information Management Systems
Corporation
2201 Hangar Place
Allentown 18103
610-264-8029; FAX: 610-264-5579

New Horizons Computer Learning
Center
125 Technology Dr.
Canonsburg 15317
412-514-5300; FAX: 412-514-5299

Inacom Information Systems
353 Markle Dr.
Harrisburg 17111
717-397-7677; FAX: 717-293-1870

Knowledge Soft, Inc.
5020 Richard Ln.
Mechanicsburg 17055
717-790-0400; FAX: 717-790-0401

Global Knowledge Network
One Allegheny Sq., Suite 102
Pittsburgh 15212-5408
412-937-4440; FAX: 412-321-2565

PC Solutions
Gatehouse, Station Sq.
Pittsburgh 15219
412-391-8830; FAX: 412-391-8488

PCDC
500 Business Center Dr.
Pittsburgh 15205
412-291-9700; FAX: 412-788-5116

XLConnect Systems, Inc.
109 Gamma Dr.
Pittsburgh 15238
412-967-6741; FAX: 412-963-9276

ECC Integrated
130 Futura Dr., P.O. Box 479
Pottstown 19464
610-495-7800 x291;
FAX: 610-495-2800

RHODE ISLAND
Roger Williams University
150 Washington St.
Computer Education Center, 2nd Fl.
Providence 02903
401-254-3500; FAX: 401-276-4862

SOUTH CAROLINA
IKON Office Solutions–Technology
Service
Trident Research Park
5300 International Blvd., Suite 102
Charleston 29418
803-553-1866; FAX: 803-935-1111

SOUTH DAKOTA
Ultra Connecting Point
3300 W 49th St., P.O. Box 88207
Sioux Falls 57106
605-361-8881; FAX: 605-361-5177

TENNESSEE
New Horizons Computer Learning
Center
3959 Volunteer Dr. A-5
P.O. Box 23346
Chattanooga 37416
423-892-3085 x139;
FAX: 423-954-1786

Bailey Computing Technologies, Inc.
926 W. Oakland Ave., Suite 214
Johnson City 37604
423-283-0543; FAX: 423-282-8887

Federal Express Corporation
2842 Business Park Dr., Bldg. G
Memphis 38118-2823
901-369-3024; FAX: 901-797-6320

New Horizons Computer Learning
Center
2600 Thousand Oaks Blvd., Suite 1300
Memphis 38118
901-375-1533; FAX: 901-375-1766

ATHENA Computer Learning Center, Inc.
501 Great Circle Rd., Suite 150
Nashville 37228
615-244-1681; FAX: 615-244-1685

XLConnect
Greenbriar Business Park
2525 Perimeter Place Dr., Suite 210
Nashville 37214
615-391-1909; FAX: 615-885-2591

TEXAS
Harding Group, Inc.
2012 E. Randol Mill Rd., Suite 216
Arlington 76011
817-461-3393; FAX: 817-461-3394

Austin Data
Spicewood Springs Rd.
Austin 78759
512-794-8455; FAX: 512-794-0536

Infotec Commercial Systems
9420 Research Blvd., Bldg. 3, Suite 200
Austin 78759
512-346-8110; FAX: 512-795-0559

New Horizons Computer Learning
Center
4515 Steton Center Pkwy., Suite 250
Austin 78759
512-349-9555 x2441;
FAX: 512-349-2316

Software Academy, Inc.
4901 LBJ Frwy., Suite 200
Dallas 75244
972-788-1694; FAX: 972-490-9633

New Horizons Computer Learning
Center
201 Main St., Suite 1100
Fort Worth 76102
817-336-9600; FAX: 817-336-5280

C-Trec
1700 West Loop S., Suite 1100
Houston 77027
713-871-8411; FAX: 713-622-1915

New Horizons Computer Learning
Center
5555 San Felipe, Suite 1500
Houston 77056
713-552-1414 x250; FAX: 713-552-0632

Infotec Commercial Systems
University Place
1651 N. Collins, Suite 125
Richardson 75081
800-234-4734 x338;
FAX: 214-644-7673

Infotec Commercial
NW Loop 410, Suite 105
San Antonio 78213
210-340-2235; FAX: 512-346-8110

New Horizons Computer Learning
Center
8200 West IH-10 Suite 120
San Antonio 78230
210-308-8200; FAX: 210-349-8269

UTAH
IKON Office Solutions–Technology
Service
455 E. 500 S.
Salt Lake City 84111
801-366-5366; FAX: 801-366-5156

Knowledge Alliance, Inc.
472 Bear Cat Dr.
Salt Lake City 84115
801-467-0400; FAX: 801-467-8383

PC Training West, LLC
2144 S. Highland Dr., Suite 180
Salt Lake City 84106
801-484-9891; FAX: 801-467-9129

VIRGINIA
America's Computer Training Source,
Inc.
191 New Market Fair, Suite 15
Newport News 23605
757-340-1111; FAX: 757-486-1520

A-Plus Computer Education, Inc.
2807 N. Parham Rd., Suite 354
Richmond 23294
804-527-0311; FAX: 804-527-0214

Computer Education Services, Inc.
7110 Forest Ave, Suite 203
Richmond 23226
804-673-1930; FAX: 804-673-2733

America's Computer Training Source, Inc.
3333-28 Virginia Beach Blvd.
Virginia Beach 23452
757-340-1111; FAX: 757-486-1520

Computer Education Services, Inc.
5701 Thurston Ave.
Virginia Beach 23455
757-460-7800; FAX: 757-464-1373

WASHINGTON
Infotec Commercial Systems
2300 130th Ave. NE, Suite 200
Bellevue 98005
800-234-4734; FAX: 425-869-4065

Capital Business Machines, Inc.
3660 Pacific Ave., P.O. Box 1456
Olympia 98501
360-491-6000; FAX: 360-438-0969

CompUSA, Inc.
Two Union Square, Suite 1717
Seattle 98101
206-382-1366; FAX: 206-382-7303

Olivetti North America
East 9922 Montgomery Bay 9
Spokane 99206
509-927-4049; FAX: 509-927-4040

WEST VIRGINIA
Riverhead Training, Inc.
300 Capitol St.,
420 Kanawha Valley Bldg.
Charleston 25301
304-345-7740; FAX: 304-345-7743

WISCONSIN
Allied Computer Group, Inc.
3011 E. Capitol Dr.
Appleton 54911
414-734-5666; FAX: 414-734-5833

Entre Computer Center
13400 Bishops Ln., Suite 270
Brookfield 53005
414-938-2139; FAX: 414-938-2155

Lanmaster Training Center
933 Anderson Dr., Suite JK
Green Bay 54304
800-844-7120; FAX: 414-498-6238

Valcom/More Than Computers, Inc.
3113 W. Beltline Hwy.
Madison 53713
608-288-2868; FAX: 608-288-2870

Allied Computer Group, Inc.
600 West Virginia St.
Milwaukee 53024
414-223-0150; FAX: 414-223-1639

IKON Office Solutions–Technology Service
11425 W. Lake Park Dr., Suite 900
Milwaukee 53224
414-577-6600; FAX: 414-577-6659

Lanmaster Training Center
10201 W. Lincoln Ave., Suite 102
Milwaukee 53227
414-541-2570; FAX: 414-541-3598

THE INSIDE TRACK

Who:	Jane Charles
What:	Software support intern
Where:	Missouri
How much:	$18,000 per year

Insider's Advice

Learn as much as you can about what interests you and be willing to work hard. Constantly try to get access to new technology that you can look at and try out so that you will be familiar with it. Before I got this internship, I would go to Kinko's and buy computer time just to have a chance to learn the new software on their system. The time I spent on the computer there gave me the hands-on experience I needed to get this job.

Try to spend as much time as you can talking to people who know more than you do. My local chamber of commerce holds free business events several times a year. I go to meet people and learn about upcoming jobs and changes in the market. And it's fun too.

Insider's Take on the Future

I don't make much money at the internship, but I'm gaining even more experience so that I can get a good job when my internship ends. I am having a lot of fun in this job; the people are very helpful, and I am finding out that there is a lot about software support I don't know. I really hope I will get hired by this company, but if not, I know that what I've learned here will help me get another job somewhere else.

CHAPTER | 4

This chapter tells you how to determine your eligibility and gather your records before you begin the financial aid process. It explains the types of financial aid available and includes sample forms and details on filing your forms once you've completed them. Lists of resources and acronyms will help you along the financial aid path.

FINANCIAL AID FOR THE TRAINING YOU NEED

Now that you have decided that becoming a computer technician is an exciting and worthwhile career, and you have chosen a training program, you need a plan for financing your training. Investigate financial aid even if you think you might not qualify. You can qualify for aid at several different types of schools, including vocational schools that offer short-term training programs, and you can qualify even if you're attending only part time. The financial aid you'll get may be less than that for longer, full-time programs, but it still can help you pay for a portion of your computer training program.

GETTING STARTED

First of all, get a Free Application for Federal Student Aid (FAFSA) from your public library or financial aid office, or order it online at *http://www.finaid.org/finaid.html* or by calling 800-4-FED-AID. Be aware that photocopies of federal forms are not acceptable. The FAFSA determines your eligibility status for all grants and loans provided by federal or state governments and certain college or institution aid, so it is the first step in the financial aid process.

Gathering Your Records

When you apply for financial aid, your answers to certain questions will determine whether you're considered dependent on your parents and must report their income and assets as well as your own, or whether you're independent and must report only your own income and assets (and those of your spouse if you're married).

If you are a dependent student, you will need financial information from your parents to fill out the FAFSA. Read the following list to determine if you are dependent or independent according to financial aid rules. You are considered an independent student if you meet any one of the following criteria:

1. You are at least 24 years old.
2. You are married.
3. You have a dependent other than a spouse.
4. You are a graduate student or professional student.
5. You are a ward of the court or an orphan.
6. You are a veteran of the U.S. Armed Forces.

To fill out the FAFSA, gather the following documents (and if you are a dependent student, your parents' documents):

- Social Security number(s)
- income tax returns for the fiscal year that just ended, and W-2 and 1099 forms
- records of untaxed income, such as Social Security benefits, child support, welfare, pensions, military subsistence allowances, and veteran's benefits
- current bank statements and mortgage information
- last year's medical and dental expenses that weren't covered by health insurance
- investment records such as stocks, bonds, and mutual funds; bank certificates of deposit (CDs) and money market accounts statements
- business and/or farm records

Determining Your Eligibility

To receive financial aid from an accredited college's or institution's student aid program, you must be a U.S. citizen or an eligible non-citizen with a Social Security number. Refer to Immigration and Naturalization Service (INS) in the Resources section at the end of this chapter if you are not a U.S. citizen and are unsure of your eligibility.

Eligibility is a very complicated matter, but it can be simplified to the following equation: your contribution + your parents' contribution = expected family contribution (EFC). Student expense budget/cost of attendance (COA) minus EFC = your financial need.

The need analysis service or federal processor looks at the following if you are a dependent student:

- family assets, including savings, stocks and bonds, real estate investments, business/farm ownership, and trusts
- parents' age and need for retirement income
- number of children and other dependents in the family household
- number of family members in college

Cost of attendance, also called student expense budget, includes tuition and fees, books and supplies, room and board (living with parents, on campus, or off campus), transportation, personal expenses, and special expenses such as child care.

TYPES OF FINANCIAL AID

The two major types of financial aid are gift aid and self-help aid.

Gift aid (a gift that does not need to be paid back), consists of grants and scholarships. Grants are normally awarded based on financial need, whereas scholarships are almost always awarded on academic merit or special characteristics (for example, ethnic heritage, interests, parents' career, geographic location) rather than financial need. They also usually only apply to tuition and other educational expenses, not living expenses.

Self-help aid consists of loans and student employment (also called work-study). There are many types of loans, all of which you have to repay with interest. Payment schedules and interest rates vary. You can arrange to work to help pay your school bills either on your own or in partnership with your school, taking into account your field of interest.

Gift aid and self-help aid are each available on four levels: federal, state, school, and private.

You will encounter an amazing number of acronyms while applying for any type of federal financial aid. Refer to the acronym list at the end of the chapter for help. Also use the Internet as a supplemental source of information (anyone who wants to become a computer technician should be familiar with the World Wide Web!). A list of helpful Internet addresses can be found in the Resources section at the end of this chapter.

Loans: Federal, State, School, Private

Federal Loans

Perkins Loans

The Perkins Loan is for students with acute financial need, so the interest rate is low (it was 5% as of 1997). You repay your school, which lends you the money with government funds. You can borrow up to $3,000 each year, up to a total of $15,000 over the course of your undergraduate study.

The school pays you directly by check or credits your account. You have nine months after you graduate (provided you were continuously enrolled at least half time) to begin repayment, with up to 10 years to pay off the entire loan.

Stafford Loans

Stafford loans are either subsidized or unsubsidized.

- Subsidized loans (the federal government pays the interest) are awarded on a need basis—this is also called Direct Stafford Loan.
- Unsubsidized loans (you pay the interest) are awarded on request—this is also called Federal Family Education Loan (FFEL) Stafford Loan.

These loans have many borrowing limits, depending on whether you get an unsubsidized or subsidized loan, which school year you're in, the length of your program, and whether you're independent or dependent. You can have both kinds of Stafford loans at the same time, but the total loaned at any time cannot exceed $23,000. The interest rate varies but purportedly will never exceed 8.25%. There is a six-month grace period after graduation before you must start repaying the loan.

PLUS Loans (Loans for Parents)

For all other kinds of student loans, you are held responsible for payment and accountable for defaulting (even if the loan is made based on your parents' finances). But this loan is made to your parents. They must have a good credit history; you must be their dependent and be enrolled at least half time.

The borrowing limit equals your cost of attendance (COA) minus all other financial aid you're receiving. The interest rate varies, but is not to exceed 9% over the life of the loan. Your parents must begin repayment while you're still in school. There is no grace period.

Consolidation Loans

This is an umbrella term for merging all your loans into "one easy monthly payment." Details vary greatly, depending on your particular borrowing plans. Consolidation loans also can be arranged on the school and private levels.

State Loans

Many states have Web sites; you can find the same information by contacting your state's department of education. You can qualify for state loans based on your residency, your parents' residency, or the location of the school you're attending.

School Loans

You can get information on school loans only through the financial aid office at the school of your choice. Quickly become acquainted with the financial aid administrators and stay in close touch. Their full-time job is to help you with your financial aid questions.

Private Loans

Check several banks, savings and loan institutions, and credit unions for loan programs. If you are dependent, consult your parents about their financial institutions and ask them to do some footwork for you in researching borrowing opportunities.

Grants and Scholarships: Federal, State, School, Private

This is the painless money—the kind you don't have to pay back. Again, don't assume you don't qualify simply because you think your finances are in pretty good shape, especially where scholarships are concerned. You won't know how much financial aid you qualify for unless you file the forms and get the process started.

Federal Grants and Scholarships

Pell Grants

The Pell Grant provides a foundation of financial aid upon which many students build. It is completely based on financial need (see previous section, Determining Your Eligibility). You can even be enrolled less than half time to qualify. If you already have a bachelor's degree, you can't receive a Pell Grant. You will not be considered for certain other sources of financial aid if you haven't first applied for a Pell Grant.

The maximum award depends on congressional funding for that school year (July 1 to June 30). For 1996–97, the limit per student was $2,470.

Federal Supplemental Educational Opportunity Grants (FSEOG)

Priority is given to students receiving Pell Grants because it is based on exceptional financial need. The FSEOG differs from the Pell Grant in that it is not guaranteed that every student in need will receive one. Each school has only a certain amount of funds to distribute among all students with a financial need.

National Merit Scholarships

About 5,000 students each year receive a scholarship from the National Merit Scholarship Corporation based solely on academic performance in high school. If you are a high school senior with excellent grades and high scores on tests such as the ACT and SAT, this scholarship can be for you.

State Grants and Scholarships

State grants and scholarships may be specific to the state in which you are trained; the state in which you reside, even if you plan to attend another school out of state; or even the state in which your parents reside. Contact your state's Department of Education for more information.

School Grants and Scholarships

You need to know which school you'll be attending to pursue a school grant or scholarship. Once you've overcome that hurdle, immediately talk to the financial aid administrator (FAA) to find out specific details about school-based grants. The financial aid office offers a wealth of information about all student aid programs, application requirements, eligibility, advice on financial planning and debt management, advice about applying for a student loan and the associated interest rates and payment schedules, and even help with short-term loans in a financial emergency. Check it out!

Private Grants and Scholarships

It is always worthwhile to look into religious organizations, businesses, labor unions, and community and professional groups for private grants and scholarships. You can find highly specific sources of financial aid in the private sector. For example, you can obtain a scholarship for being a certain gender in a certain field, of a particular ethnicity, an athlete, or a music lover. Places to look for help include local community organizations such as the Rotary Club, American Legion, 4H Club, chamber of commerce, PTA/PTSA, and Boy Scouts and Girl Scouts. Perhaps your parents' companies offer financial aid to children of employees. Check with the personnel office. Also check with your library for directories of professional, career, and trade associations in the computer industry that offer scholarships and loans, especially if you are specializing in a certain company's software or hardware. Also check computer-related magazines. You never know what type of private aid you might dig up.

Work-Study

Your school's student employment office is the place to head for more information about work-study. Work options include on- or off-campus; part time or almost full time; in the computer field or just to pay the bills. For money to repay student loans or to go directly toward educational expenses, Americorps offers jobs that pay up to $4,725 a year (as of 1996–97).

One advantage of working under Federal Work Study (FWS) is that your earnings are exempt from FICA taxes if you are enrolled full time and are working less than half time. You will be paid by the hour, at least minimum wage. For FWS, you must demonstrate financial need. Usually you will be signed up for a community service or computer-related job in a private nonprofit organization or a public agency. Some schools have agreements with private for-profit companies, if the work demands your computer technician skills. The total hourly wages you earn cannot exceed your total FWS award. Your financial aid administrator (FAA) or the direct employer must consider your class schedule and your academic progress before assigning your job.

FILING YOUR FORMS

Start investigating financial aid as soon as possible. The FAFSA can be filed any time between January 1 and June 30; however, the closer to January 1, the better. Do not file before January 1 of the year in which you want to obtain financial aid, or your application will be discarded. You will need federal and state income tax information, but even if your parents or you haven't filed yet, you can submit the FAFSA with estimated income tax information. You may wish to mail your application by certified mail. Within four weeks after you mail the form, you should receive a Student Aid Report (SAR) detailing your eligibility. Your SAR will also be forwarded for Pell Grant evaluation and to up to six schools of your choice. If more than four weeks go by and you don't get the SAR, call the federal processor at 319-337-5665 to find out what happened. You will be asked for your Social Security number and date of birth as verification.

Your application must be received by June 30 of the school year you want to attend. The Student Aid Report (SAR) must be at your school by August 31 or your last day of enrollment of that school year, whichever is earlier.

Carefully meet any deadlines set by state, school, or private sources of financial aid. Your Financial Aid Administrator (FAA) should make these clear to you.

If all goes well, you will receive financial assistance to become a computer technician. If you get a loan, be sure you understand how the money will pay your bills—will it be paid directly to the school, deposited in your account, sent to you in check form? And just as important, be sure you understand how you are to pay back the loan. Most loans require no payment until you have completed your training. However, there are rules about staying enrolled, taking leaves of absence, grace periods after graduation, and so on. You need to investigate and take responsibility for loan repayment once you accept financial aid. Also talk to the financial aid office about spreading your payments over the school year rather than paying in a lump sum, and consolidating more than one loan into one payment.

Note that you have to reapply for financial aid every year that you are in school. Once you are started on financial aid, you should receive a renewal FAFSA by January 15 each year. Probably 75 percent of the information will remain the same from year to year, but you may need to report changes in your income, how many of your family members are in college, and your family size. Always have a copy of each year's FAFSA sent to your school's financial aid office.

Financial Aid Checklist

1. Explore your options as soon as possible after you've decided to begin a training program.

2. Find out what your school requires and what financial aid it offers.

3. Complete and mail the FAFSA as soon as possible after January 1.

4. Complete and mail other applications by the deadlines.

5. Gather loan application information and forms from your college financial aid office. You must forward the certified loan application to a participating lender: bank, savings and loan institution, or credit union.

6. Carefully read all letters and notices from the school, the federal student aid processor, the need analysis service, and private scholarship organizations. Note whether financial aid will be sent before or after you are notified about admission, and how exactly you will receive the money.

7. Report any changes in your financial resources or expenses to your financial aid office so your award can be adjusted accordingly.

8. Reapply each year.

RESOURCES
Scholarship Search Services

If you find financial aid information overwhelming, or if you simply don't have the time to do the footwork yourself, you may want to hire a scholarship search service. Be aware that a reasonable price is $30 to $50. If the service wants to charge more, investigate it carefully. Scholarship search services usually only provide you with a list of six or so sources of scholarships that you then need to check out and apply for.

If you're still in high school and you haven't yet filled out the ETS Student Search Service form or the ACT Student Profile form, check "Yes" in the box asking if you wish to release your information to scholarship programs.

Software

Cash for Class
800-205-9581; FAX: 714-673-9039
Redheads Software, Inc.
3334 East Coast Hwy. #216
Corona del Mar, CA 92625
cashclass@aol.com

C-LECT Financial Aid Module
800-622-7284; 315-497-0330; FAX: 315-497-3359
Chronicle Guidance Publications
P.O. Box 1190
Moravia, NY 13118-1190

Peterson's Award Search
800-338-3282; 609-243-9111
Peterson's
P.O. Box 2123
Princeton, NJ 08543-2123
custsvc@petersons.com

Pinnacle Peak Solutions (Scholarships 101)
800-762-7101; 602-951-9377; FAX: 602-948-7603
Pinnacle Peak Solutions
7735 East Windrose Dr.
Scottsdale, AZ 85260

TP Software–Student Financial Aid Search Software
800-791-7791; 619-496-8673
TP Software
P.O. Box 532
Bonita, CA 91908-0532
mail@tpsoftware.com

Books and Pamphlets

The Student Guide. Published by the U.S. Department of Education, this is *the* handbook about federal aid programs. To order a copy, call 800-4-FED-AID.

Looking for Student Aid. Published by the U.S. Department of Education, this is an overview of sources of information about financial aid. To order a copy, call 800-4-FED-AID.

How Can I Receive Financial Aid for College? Published from the Parent Brochures ACCESS ERIC Web site. Order a copy by calling 800-LET-ERIC or writing to ACCESS ERIC, Research Blvd. MS 5F, Rockville, MD 20850-3172.

Annual Register of Grant Support. Chicago: Marquis, Annual.

A's and B's of Academic Scholarships. Alexandria, VA: Octameron, Annual.

Chronicle Student Aid Annual. Moravia, NY: Chronicle Guidance, Annual.

College Blue Book. Scholarships, Fellowships, Grants and Loans. New York: MacMillan, Annual.

College Financial Aid Annual. New York: Prentice-Hall, Annual.

Directory of Financial Aids for Minorities and *Directory of Financial Aids for Women.* San Carlos, CA: Reference Service Press, Biennial.

Don't Miss Out: The Ambitious Student's Guide to Financial Aid. Robert and Ann Leider. Alexandria, VA: Octameron, Annual.

Financial Aids for Higher Education. Dubuque: Wm. C. Brown, Biennial.

Financial Aid for the Disabled and their Families. San Carlos, CA: Reference Service Press, Biennial.

Paying Less for College. Princeton: Peterson's Guides, Annual.

Telephone Numbers and Addresses

Federal Student Aid Information Center
P.O. Box 84, Washington, DC 20044
319-337-5665
TDD 800-730-8913

800-4-FED-AID (800-433-3243) 9 a.m.–8 p.m. ET, M–F

800-MIS-USED (800-647-8733) for suspicion of fraud, waste, or abuse of federal aid.

ACT American College Testing program, 916-361-0656, for forms submitted to the need analysis servicer.

College Scholarship Service (CSS), 609-771-7725; TDD 609-883-7051

Need Access/Need Analysis Service, 800-282-1550

Selective Service, 847-688-6888

Immigration and Naturalization Services (INS), 415-705-4205

Internal Revenue Service (IRS), 800-829-1040

Social Security Administration, 800-772-1213

National and Community Service Program (Americorps), 800-94-ACORPS

FAFSA on the WEB Processing/Software Problems, 800-801-0576

For telephone numbers specific to loan programs, loan consolidations, tuition payment plans, and state prepaid tuition plans, access *http://www.finaid.org/finaid/phone.html*

Web Sites

- *One of the most comprehensive Web sites is http://www.finaid.org/finaid.* It has many pages addressing special situations, such as international students, bankruptcy, defaulting on student loans, divorced parents, financially unsupportive parents, and myths about financial aid.

- Another equally excellent Web site is FastWEB at *http://www.fastweb.com.* If you answer a few simple questions (such as geographical location and age), you will receive a list of scholarships for which you may qualify. Their database is updated regularly, and your list will be updated when new scholarships are added that fit your profile. FastWEB boasts that every day more than 20,000 students access the site.

- Software for EFC calculators and financial aid planning and advice can be found at *http://www.finaid.org/finaid/vendors/software.html*

- Free online documents can be found at *http://www.finaid.org/finaid/documents.html*

Financial Aid Acronyms Key

COA	Cost of Attendance
CWS	College Work-Study
EFC	Expected Family Contribution
EFT	Electronic Funds Transfer
ESAR	Electronic Student Aid Report
ETS	Educational Testing Service
FAA	Financial Aid Administrator
FAF	Financial Aid Form
FAFSA	Free Application for Federal Student Aid
FAO	Financial Aid Office
FDSLP	Federal Direct Student Loan Program
FFELP	Federal Family Education Loan Program
FSEOG	Federal Supplemental Educational Opportunity Grant
FWS	Federal Work-Study
GSL	Guaranteed Student Loan
PC	Parent Contribution
PLUS	Parent Loan for Undergraduate Students
SAP	Satisfactory Academic Progress
SC	Student Contribution
SLS	Supplemental Loan for Students
USED	U.S. Department of Education

*F*ree *A*pplication *for F*ederal *S*tudent *A*id
1997–98 School Year

WARNING: If you purposely give false or misleading information on this form, you may be fined $10,000, sent to prison, or both.

"You" and "your" on this form always mean the student who wants aid.

Form Approved
OMB No. 1840-0110
App. Exp. 6/30/98

U.S. Department of Education
Student Financial
Assistance Programs

Use dark ink. Make capital letters and numbers clear and legible.   `E X M 2 4`   *Fill in ovals completely. Only one oval per question.*   Correct ●   *Incorrect marks will be ignored.*   Incorrect ⊗ ✓

SAMPLE

Section A: You (the student)

1–3. Your name

1. Last name   2. First name   3. M.I.

Your title (optional)   Mr. ○ 1   Miss, Mrs., or Ms. ○ 2

4–7. Your permanent mailing address (*All mail will be sent to this address. See Instructions, page 2 for state/country abbreviations.*)

4. Number and street (Include apt. no.)

5. City   6. State   7. ZIP code

8. Your social security number (SSN) (*Don't leave blank. See Instructions, page 2.*)

9. Your date of birth   Month Day Year   1 9

10. Your permanent home telephone number   Area code

11. Your state of legal residence   State

12. Date you became a legal resident of the state in question 11 (*See Instructions, page 2.*)   Month Day Year   1 9

13–14. Your driver's license number (*Include the state abbreviation. If you don't have a license, write in "None."*)
State   License number

15–16. Are you a U.S. citizen? (*See Instructions, pages 2–3.*)
Yes, I am a U.S. citizen.   ○ 1
No, but I am an eligible noncitizen.   ○ 2
A
No, neither of the above.   ○ 3

17. As of today, are you married? (*Fill in only one oval.*)
I am not married. (I am single, widowed, or divorced.)   ○ 1
I am married.   ○ 2
I am separated from my spouse.   ○ 3

18. Date you were married, separated, divorced, or widowed. If divorced, use date of divorce or separation, whichever is earlier. (*If never married, leave blank.*)   Month Year   1 9

19. Will you have your first bachelor's degree before July 1, 1997?   Yes ○ 1   No ○ 2

Section B: Education Background

20–21. Date that you (the student) received, or will receive, your high school diploma, either— (*Enter one date. Leave blank if the question does not apply to you.*)

- by graduating from high school   **20.**   Month Year   1 9
  OR
- by earning a GED   **21.**   Month Year   1 9

22–23. Highest educational level or grade level your father and your mother completed. (*Fill in one oval for each parent. See Instructions, page 3.*)

	22. Father	23. Mother
elementary school (K–8)	○ 1	○ 1
high school (9–12)	○ 2	○ 2
college or beyond	○ 3	○ 3
unknown	○ 4	○ 4

If you (and your family) have **unusual circumstances**, complete this form and then check with your financial aid administrator. Examples:
- tuition expenses at an elementary or secondary school,
- unusual medical or dental expenses not covered by insurance,
- a family member who recently became unemployed, or
- other unusual circumstances such as changes in income or assets that might affect your eligibility for student financial aid.

Section C: Your Plans *Answer these questions about your college plans.* *Page 2*

24–28. Your expected enrollment status for the 1997–98 school year
(See Instructions, page 3.)

School term	Full time	3/4 time	1/2 time	Less than 1/2 time	Not enrolled
24. Summer term '97	○ 1	○ 2	○ 3	○ 4	○ 5
25. Fall semester/qtr. '97	○ 1	○ 2	○ 3	○ 4	○ 5
26. Winter quarter '97-98	○ 1	○ 2	○ 3	○ 4	○ 5
27. Spring semester/qtr. '98	○ 1	○ 2	○ 3	○ 4	○ 5
28. Summer term '98	○ 1	○ 2	○ 3	○ 4	○ 5

29. Your course of study *(See Instructions for code, page 3.)* Code ☐

30. College degree/certificate you expect to receive *(See Instructions for code, page 3.)* ☐

31. Date you expect to receive your degree/certificate   Month Day Year ☐

32. Your grade level during the 1997–98 school year *(Fill in only one.)*

- 1st yr./never attended college ○ 1
- 1st yr./attended college before ○ 2
- 2nd year/sophomore ○ 3
- 3rd year/junior ○ 4
- 4th year/senior ○ 5
- 5th year/other undergraduate ○ 6
- 1st year graduate/professional ○ 7
- 2nd year graduate/professional ○ 8
- 3rd year graduate/professional ○ 9
- Beyond 3rd year graduate/professional ○ 10

33–35. In addition to grants, what other types of financial aid are you (and your parents) interested in? *(See Instructions, page 3.)*

33. Student employment   Yes ○ 1   No ○ 2
34. Student loans   Yes ○ 1   No ○ 2
35. Parent loans for students   Yes ○ 1   No ○ 2

36. If you are (or were) in college, do you plan to attend that **same college** in 1997–98? *(If this doesn't apply to you, leave blank.)*   Yes ○ 1   No ○ 2

37. For how many dependents will you (the student) pay child care or elder care expenses in 1997–98? ☐

38–39. Veterans education benefits you expect to receive from July 1, 1997 through June 30, 1998

38. Amount per month $ ☐ .00
39. Number of months ☐

Section D: Student Status

40. Were you born **before** January 1, 1974? .... Yes ○ 1   No ○ 2
41. Are you a veteran of the U.S. Armed Forces? ...... Yes ○ 1   No ○ 2
42. Will you be enrolled in a graduate or professional program (beyond a bachelor's degree) in 1997-98? ...... Yes ○ 1   No ○ 2
43. Are you married? .... Yes ○ 1   No ○ 2
44. Are you an orphan or a ward of the court, or **were** you a ward of the court until age 18? ...... Yes ○ 1   No ○ 2
45. Do you have legal dependents (**other than a spouse**) that fit the definition in Instructions, page 4? ...... Yes ○ 1   No ○ 2

If you answered **"Yes"** to any question in Section D, go to Section E and fill out **both the GRAY and the WHITE** areas on the rest of this form.

If you answered **"No"** to **every** question in Section D, go to Section E and fill out **both the GREEN and the WHITE** areas on the rest of this form.

Section E: Household Information

Remember:
At least one "Yes" answer in Section D means fill out the **GRAY** and WHITE areas.

All "No" answers in Section D means fill out the **GREEN** and WHITE areas.

STUDENT (& SPOUSE)

46. Number in your household in 1997–98 *(Include yourself and your spouse. Do not include your children and other people unless they meet the definition in Instructions, page 4.)* ☐

47. Number of college students in household in 1997–98 *(Of the number in 46, how many will be in college at least half-time in at least one term in an eligible program? Include yourself. See Instructions, page 4.)* ☐

PARENT(S)

48. Your parent(s)' **current** marital status:
single ○ 1   separated ○ 3   widowed ○ 5
married ○ 2   divorced ○ 4

49. Your parent(s)' state of legal residence   State ☐

50. Date your parent(s) became legal resident(s) of the state in question 49 *(See Instructions, page 5.)*   Month Day Year 1 9

51. Number in your parent(s)' household in 1997–98 *(Include yourself and your parents. Do not include your parents' other children and other people unless they meet the definition in Instructions, page 5.)* ☐

52. Number of college students in household in 1997–98 *(Of the number in 51, how many will be in college at least half-time in at least one term in an eligible program? Include yourself. See Instructions, page 5.)* ☐

Section F: 1996 Income, Earnings, and Benefits *You must see Instructions, pages 5 and 6, for information about* *Page 3* *tax forms and tax filing status, especially if you are estimating taxes or filing electronically or by telephone. These instructions will tell you what income and benefits should be reported in this section.*

	STUDENT (& SPOUSE)	PARENT(S)

The following 1996 U.S. income tax figures are from:

53. *(Fill in one oval.)* — Everyone must fill out this column.

65. *(Fill in one oval.)*

A—a completed 1996 IRS Form 1040A, 1040EZ, or 1040TEL .... ○ 1 A .... ○ 1

B—a completed 1996 IRS Form 1040 .... ○ 2 B .... ○ 2

C—an estimated 1996 IRS Form 1040A, 1040EZ, or 1040TEL .... ○ 3 C .... ○ 3

D—an estimated 1996 IRS Form 1040 .... ○ 4 D .... ○ 4

E—will not file a 1996 U.S. income tax return .... *(Skip to question 57.)* ○ 5 E *(Skip to 69.)* ○ 5

1996 Total number of exemptions (Form 1040–line 6d, or 1040A–line 6d; 1040EZ filers— *see Instructions, page 6.*) **54.** / **66.**

1996 Adjusted Gross Income (AGI: Form 1040–line 31, 1040A–line 16, or 1040EZ–line 4 *see Instructions, page 6.*) **55.** $ .00 / **67.** $ .00

1996 U.S. income tax **paid** (Form 1040–line 44, 1040A–line 25, or 1040EZ–line 10) **56.** $ .00 / **68.** $ .00

TAX FILERS ONLY

1996 Income earned from work (Student) **57.** $ .00 (Father) **69.** $ .00

1996 Income earned from work (Spouse) **58.** $ .00 (Mother) **70.** $ .00

1996 Untaxed income and benefits (yearly totals only):

Earned Income Credit (Form 1040–line 54, Form 1040A–line 29c, or Form 1040EZ–line 8) **59.** $ .00 / **71.** $ .00

Untaxed Social Security Benefits **60.** $ .00 / **72.** $ .00

Aid to Families with Dependent Children (AFDC/ADC) **61.** $ .00 / **73.** $ .00

Child support received for all children **62.** $ .00 / **74.** $ .00

Other untaxed income and benefits from Worksheet #2, page 11 **63.** $ .00 / **75.** $ .00

1996 Amount from Line 5, Worksheet #3, page 12 *(See Instructions.)* **64.** $ .00 / **76.** $ .00

Section G: Asset Information   **ATTENTION!**

Fill out Worksheet A or Worksheet B in Instructions, page 7. *If you meet the tax filing and income conditions on Worksheets A and B, you do not have to complete Section G to apply for Federal student aid. Some states and colleges, however, require Section G information for their own aid programs. Check with your financial aid administrator and/or State Agency.*

Age of your older parent **84.**

	STUDENT (& SPOUSE)	PARENT(S)

Cash, savings, and checking accounts **77.** $ .00 / **85.** $ .00

Other real estate and investments value *(Don't include the home.)* **78.** $ .00 / **86.** $ .00

Other real estate and investments debt *(Don't include the home.)* **79.** $ .00 / **87.** $ .00

Business value **80.** $ .00 / **88.** $ .00

Business debt **81.** $ .00 / **89.** $ .00

Investment farm value *(See Instructions, page 8.)* *(Don't include a family farm.)* **82.** $ .00 / **90.** $ .00

Investment farm debt *(See Instructions, page 8.)* *(Don't include a family farm.)* **83.** $ .00 / **91.** $ .00

Section H: Releases and Signatures

92–103. What college(s) do you plan to attend in 1997–98?
(Note: The colleges you list below will have access to your application information. See Instructions, page 8.)

Housing codes	1—on-campus	3—with parent(s)
	2—off-campus	4—with relative(s) other than parent(s)

Title IV School Code	College Name	College Street Address and City	State	Housing Code
XX. 0 5 4 3 2 1	EXAMPLE UNIVERSITY	14930 NORTH SOMEWHERE BLVD. ANYWHERE CITY	S T XX.	2
92.				93.
94.				95.
96.				97.
98.				99.
100.				101.
102.				103.

104. The U.S. Department of Education will send information from this form to your state financial aid agency and the state agencies of the colleges listed above so they can consider you for state aid. Answer **"No"** if you **don't** want information released to the state. *(See Instructions, page 9 and "Deadlines for State Student Aid," page 10.)* .... 104. No ◯ 2

105. Males not yet registered for Selective Service (SS): Do you want SS to register you? *(See Instructions, page 9.)* ...... 105. Yes ◯ 1

106–107. Read, Sign, and Date Below

All of the information provided by me or any other person on this form is true and complete to the best of my knowledge. I understand that this application is being filed jointly by all signatories. If asked by an authorized official, I agree to give proof of the information that I have given on this form. I realize that this proof may include a copy of my U.S. or state income tax return. I also realize that if I do not give proof when asked, the student may be denied aid.

Statement of Educational Purpose. I certify that I will use any Federal Title IV, HEA funds I receive during the award year covered by this application solely for expenses related to my attendance at the institution of higher education that determined or certified my eligibility for those funds.

Certification Statement on Overpayments and Defaults. I understand that I may not receive any Federal Title IV, HEA funds if I owe an overpayment on any Title IV educational grant or loan or am in default on a Title IV educational loan unless I have made satisfactory arrangements to repay or otherwise resolve the overpayment or default. I also understand that I must notify my school if I do owe an overpayment or am in default.

Everyone whose information is given on this form should sign below. The student (and at least one parent, if parental information is given) must sign below or this form will be returned unprocessed.

106. Signatures   *(Sign in the boxes below.)*

1 Student

2 Student's Spouse

3 Father/Stepfather

4 Mother/Stepmother

107. Date completed   Month Day Year   1997 ◯   1998 ◯

Section I: Preparer's Use Only

For preparers other than student, spouse, and parent(s). Student, spouse, and parent(s), sign in question 106.

Preparer's name (last, first, MI)

Firm name

Firm or preparer's address (street, city, state, ZIP)

108. Employer identification number (EIN)
OR
109. Preparer's social security number

Certification: All of the information on this form is true and complete to the best of my knowledge.

110. **Preparer's signature**   **Date**

School Use Only

D/O ◯   Title IV Code

FAA Signature

MDE Use Only *Do not write in this box*   Special handle

MAKE SURE THAT YOU HAVE COMPLETED, DATED, AND SIGNED THIS APPLICATION.
Mail the original application (NOT A PHOTOCOPY) to: Federal Student Aid Programs, P.O. Box 4008, Mt. Vernon, IL 62864-8608

Who:	Ellen Stein
What:	Help desk technician
Where:	California
How much:	$31,000 per year

Insider's Advice

I got my technician jobs through contract houses for about a year. I really appreciated having someone else who was out looking for my next job when I was nearing the end of a contract; it put my mind at ease.

I started at this company on a three-month contract. They were happy with my work and renewed my contract for another six months. After that, they offered me a full-time job. I would not have gotten into this company if I hadn't been contracting—they made the initial contacts for me.

Insider's Take on the Future

My company really encourages its employees to grow and learn. They have allotted $1,500 a year for each employee to attend classes or seminars that will make them better employees. I can't wait. My goal is to attend three seminars and one class at our local college. This is exactly the type of job I wanted; I would highly recommend contracting to anyone!

CHAPTER | 5

This chapter explains how to find a job after you complete your training program. First you'll learn how to conduct your job search through networking, researching the field, reading industry publications, and using classified ads, online resources, job fairs, and hotlines. Then you'll get tips on how to write your resume and cover letter and how to ace your interview.

HOW TO LAND YOUR FIRST JOB

Now that you've completed your training program, you are ready to go. On your mark, get set, now what? The job hunt! The good news is that there are a lot of available jobs in the computer industry because it's a booming field. You will find more than just a job; you will find a job that is a good fit for you.

CONDUCTING YOUR JOB SEARCH

Finding the right job always begins with research. Luckily, a lot of material is available to guide your search. By using techniques ranging from answering classified ads and networking to attending job fairs and using the Internet, you can confidently land your first job as a computer technician. Read on for keys to maximizing your job hunting success.

Knowing the Extent of the Field

Many job seekers limit their potential success by limiting their job search. Keep in mind that almost every industry requires computer technicians.

Schools, hospitals, publishers, banks, and design firms all use computers and all hire computer technicians. Restricting your search to the computer industry may keep you from a dream job in the healthcare industry.

Start your job search by making a list of all the fields that interest you. Then think about the type of environment you might feel most comfortable working in: a large national company with a corporate environment, a small startup company with a family feel, or something in between.

Classified Ads

The classified ads are an easy and inexpensive way to job hunt; the paper comes right to your doorstep, and it contains pages of job openings geared to computer professionals. When you use the classified ads as a resource, look in the computer section for job titles such as technician, support, repair, network, and desktop.

The problem with relying solely on the classified ads for your job search is that the same paper that comes to your doorstep also arrives at the doorsteps of several thousand of your neighbors. For every job listed, dozens of applicants will send a resume to the employer, and you will be competing with all of them. Don't ignore the ads; just know that you need to use additional job search strategies to maximize your success.

Following are examples of recent classified ads seeking computer technicians in a variety of areas.

Help Desk Technician

This position is responsible for request management and assignment, user account control, and documentation and reporting. Customer-support orientation and desire to work on multiple projects required. Working knowledge of asset management and software testing valued. The qualified candidate will have a two- or four-year degree with one-plus years of related experience.

PC Technician

Major responsibilities: install, maintain, and troubleshoot networked PC hardware and software including NT, DOS, OS/2, and Windows for Workgroups; develop and maintain client configuration procedures for the Technical Procedure Manual; assist in maintaining the database for hardware/software inventories and help desk. Requirements: technical certificate and/or equivalent experience, hardware troubleshooting expertise, intermediate to advanced Windows NT or Windows 95 skills, excellent organizational skills. Knowledge of network peripherals and MS Office Pro applications and Novell IntranetWare client experience desired.

Computer Technician

Two to three years of experience in PC installations, troubleshooting, and break/fix hardware and software. A+ certification a requirement. Other manufacturers certification a plus. Growth opportunities unlimited. Wages commensurate with experience and certification.

Microcomputer Technician

Temporary position. Assist in installation and maintenance of office hardware and software and assist users with computer-related problems. Requirement: two years of computer training, one year related experience, or equivalent combination of education and experience.

HelpDesk

Full-time individual to assist users with PC applications, monitor systems/operations. UNIX, Windows, LAN environment. Two-year degree or job-related experience.

Computer Technicians

We are looking for qualified laptop and desktop repair technicians with a minimum of one to two years of experience in Compaq, IBM, Apple, Packard-Bell, AST, NEC, etc. Responsible for troubleshooting, repair, and testing. Must be able to upgrade hardware and software and have knowledge of DOS, Windows, and utilities programs.

Computer Technician Assistant

Full-time. Ideal candidate must be proficient in Windows 95, Novell, and various software programs. Technical degree required. Must be reliable, diligent, have excellent problem-solving skills, and be able to work independently. Salary commensurate with experience.

Computer Technician/Support

Assemble computer systems and provide customer hardware/software support. Requirements: dependable, professional, thorough knowledge of Windows 95.

Information Center Specialist

Technical specialist to install and configure our micro-PCs along with their corresponding peripherals and operating systems. You will also be responsible for hardware and software evaluation, consulting, and troubleshooting. Requirements: three years of experience in microprocessor hardware and software installation, troubleshooting, technical support, and training. We also require one year of experience with LAN and in-depth knowledge of Windows and Office. Background in computer sciences or ISS.

LAN Technician

Opening for an individual with strong data communications, 4.11 Novell administration, and PC hardware support. Writes UNIX shell scripts to supply system management, provides phone support for the installation of PC applications. Windows 95 and MS Office required.

Internet Technician

Qualified candidate will have a CNE and have proven experience in creating and maintaining a multiserver Novell LAN with integrated NT and UNIX servers. Experience with Microsoft Backoffice, Web servers, WANs, remote access, and remote management of network and client equipment.

PC System Support Specialist

Responsible for supporting and maintaining all PCs and assisting the network specialist in supporting network components and LAN communications systems. Install all PC hardware, software, printers, and peripherals. Perform upgrades and patches to all PC hardware and software. Provide end-user support and training as needed. Qualifications include a two-year technical degree and minimum two years of experience. Candidate must be proficient in network connectivity issues, PC hardware, and DOS, Win 95, and NT.

Computer Support Technician

Candidate should have current experience with a Novell 4 network environment, Windows 95, and Windows NT workstations. Experience with NorTel Meridian PBX phone system and voice mail are pluses. Position requires strong problem-solving skills as a technician; must work well in a team environment. Support team is responsible for both hardware and software of a midsize LAN, workstations, and user support.

Job Directories

The library and local chamber of commerce maintain directories of employers in your area. Two excellent sources organized specifically for job hunters are *The World Almanac National Job Finder's Guide* (St. Martin's Press) and the *Job Bank* series (Adams, Inc.). There are brief job descriptions and online resources in the *Job Finder's Guide;* the *Job Bank* books are published by geographic region and contain a section profiling specific companies, with contact information for major employers in your region sorted by industry. Once you've identified companies in your area of interest, use the resources at your local library to learn more about them. Your librarian can help you find public information about local firms, including the names of all the company's officers, the number of employees, a brief description of the company, and contact information.

School Career Placement Centers

Many colleges, universities, and technical schools have a career guidance office that receives job openings from a variety of local employers. Many of these guidance offices also offer resume-writing assistance and interview skills training. If you have access to one, make use of it.

Online Resources

One of the fastest growing resources for job searching is the Internet. Companies of all sizes now have Web sites that describe their business and list job openings. In addition, the federal government, many state and local governments, and several national job banks have Web sites with thousands of job listings all over the country. Most libraries and many schools allow free Internet access to their patrons. In fact, the Public Library Association has published its own *Guide to Internet Job Searching*. This book contains an entire section devoted to search techniques for the Internet that will help you find exactly what you are looking for.

If you are interested in working for a particular company, use the Internet search for its Web site and find out if it posts job openings. If you are looking for a government job, check out http:\\www.jobsfed.com. This site lists over 10,000 federal jobs. Also search the Internet to see if your state's placement office has a Web site. Not all states have a Web site, but most do. The URL (uniform resource locator) address for most of these sites follows this format: http://www.*two-letter abbreviation for the state*.state.pub (example: http://www.*mn*.state.pub or http://www.*ny*.state.pub).

Useful online resources for job searching are listed on the next page.

Job Placement Firms

Generally speaking, two types of businesses specialize in job placement: employment agencies and contract houses. Employment agencies search for full-time employment opportunities for you. Sometimes you are required to pay their fee; sometimes your new employer will pay it. Be sure to find out who is responsible for paying the fee before you sign up with an agency. After you are placed in a job, your relationship with the placement agency ends.

A contract house places you in short- or long-term contract positions for an ongoing fee paid by the employer (example: the employer pays $20 per hour for your skills; you make $15 per hour, and the contract house makes $5 per hour). When your contract with a particular company is over, the contract house finds

Job-Related Web Sites

URL and Name	Fee or No Fee	Job Postings	Entry-level Jobs	Computer Jobs	Company Profiles	Salary Survey	Resume Postings	Career Advice	Job Fairs
http://www.careermosaic.com **Career Mosaic**	No Fee	X	X	X	X		X	X	X
http://www.espan.com **e.span**	No Fee	X		X	X		X	X	X
http://iccWeb.com/employ.html **Internet Career Connection**	Fee	X	X	X			$25 / resume	X	
http://www.hoovers.com **Hoover's Online**	No Fee				X				
http://www.intellimatch.com **Intellimatch**	No Fee	X	X	X			X		X
http://www.jobbankusa.com **Job Bank USA**	No Fee	X	X	X			X	X	
http://www.monster.com **The Monster Board**	No Fee	X	X	X	X		X	X	X
http://www.occ.com **Online Career Center**	No Fee	X	X	X			X	X	X
http://jobsource.com **JobSource**	No Fee							X	
http://www.zdnet.com/zdimag/salaryzone/ **Salary Zone**	No Fee					X		X	
http://www.careersite.com/ **Career Site**	No Fee	X	X	X	X				
http://www.collegeview.com **College View**	No Fee					X		X	

another contract position for you. You are not an employee of the companies you contract with, and you do not receive benefits from them. An advantage of contracting is that you get a variety of experiences.

Job Fairs

Attending job fairs, or career fairs, is another way to find employment as a computer technician. Held at least once a year in most larger cities, job fairs bring together a number of employers under one roof, usually a convention center or civic center. These employers send representatives to the fair to inform prospective employees about their company, to accept resumes, and, occasionally, to conduct interviews for open positions. Most of these job fairs also hold seminars for attendees covering such topics as resume writing, job hunting strategies, and interviewing skills.

To find the next scheduled job fair in your area, contact the information office of the convention center or civic center nearest you and ask if there's a job fair on their upcoming events calendar. If not, the local newspaper or state unemployment office may have relevant information.

Job Hotlines

Many companies maintain a list of job openings through telephone hotlines. These job hotlines are a great way to find jobs with specific companies without having to contact the human resources department directly. Using a touch-tone telephone, you can listen to a company's list of available jobs and requirements. Job hotlines usually are not found in the phone book, but *The National Job Hotline Directory*, updated every year, lists thousands of job hotlines all over the country, including those for the state and federal government. It is available at most local libraries and bookstores.

Industry News

Knowing how to stay on top of changes in your field will help make you a more attractive candidate for any job. One of the best ways to track industry changes and identify industry trends is by reading newspapers and publications geared toward that industry. These publications will announce breaking news for the industry and explain its significance. Being up on industry news will help convince potential employers that you will be a valuable asset to their company.

You need to watch two types of trends: those specific to the computer industry and those specific to the company/industry you want to work in. Articles in computer-related magazines, e-zines (online magazines), and journals can help you keep up with emerging trends in the computer industry. Your knowledge of trends—the direction of future computer development—will make you more noticeable as a prospective employee and more valuable as a full-time employee. You will bring a strategic vision to your position based on your informed insight about the trends of the future. See Appendix B for a list of relevant computer magazines.

You also need to be aware of trends in the industry or company of your choice (medical, state universities, banks, and so on). For instance, an article in the business section of your local newspaper announcing a new vice president may signal that the company is either expanding or changing direction and might soon be hiring new employees. An article in your area's business newspaper describing the legislature's plans to impose a new law that will affect local businesses might lead you to either approach or avoid those companies in your job search. A series of articles in an industry publication about the future of business in that industry should help you focus your job-hunting strategy.

Networking

You've heard the expression "It's not what you know, it's who you know." To be honest, it's both. What you know is vital to getting a job; who you know can also help.

What is Networking?

Networking is simply getting to know people in your industry and maintaining contact with them. Networking relationships can provide many benefits:

* mentoring
* contacts within a prospective employment company
* information about emerging technology
* cutting-edge training
* information about trends in the industry

Getting Good Contacts

How do you begin networking? You probably already have. Any time you talk to someone you meet about your mutual interests in the computer field or emerging technology, you have made a contact. Of course, the contact will be short-lived if the person walks away before you get a name and phone number. Make a habit of exchanging business cards with people you meet in your field. You can get your own business cards even before you land your first job. Include your name, phone number, and a title, such as computer technician or computer repair person.

However, you don't want to exchange cards with everyone you meet. You'll run out of your own cards and places to store all the cards you collect. So whom should you consider a contact? Mainly people you meet through family and friends who work in the computer field, especially if they have experience you can learn from. Exchange cards with people in a position to hire new computer technicians. And don't discount your peers—consider peers who are energetic, personally motivated, and advancing in their field as good contacts too.

Expanding Your Contact List

If a computer professional speaks to one of your classes or you take a seminar from a working professional, ask for his or her business card. Ask the person a few questions, and then follow up the next day with a phone call or email, saying thank you or asking an additional question.

Also consider requesting informational interviews at companies that interest you. An informational interview is one in which you meet with someone to find out about the company—what it does, what sorts of positions are available or may be in the future. This is discussed further in the Interview section later in this chapter. An informational interview is an excellent opportunity for you in many ways:

- You learn more about how companies work.
- You gain interview experience.
- You gain a contact that might help you get a job in the future.

Maintaining Your Contacts

It is important to maintain contacts once you have established them. Try to contact people again within two weeks of meeting them. You can always send a note of thanks, ask a question, or send a piece of information related to your conversation with them. This contact cements your meeting in their minds; they will remember you more readily when you contact them again. If you haven't been in contact with some people for a few months, you might send them a note or email about a relevant new technology or article you read. Keep your name fresh in their minds.

Organizing Your Contact List

Many software packages can help you maintain your contact list. Or use business cards on a Rolodex or a list in your day planner. Either way, try to maintain the following pieces of information about each person:

- name
- address
- email address
- phone number(s)
- fax number
- company

- position
- first meeting (where, when, what topics did you discuss?)
- last contact (when, why, and how)

WRITING YOUR RESUME

What Goes in a Resume?

Most potential employers want to know the same basic things about you: your name/address, education/training, computer skills, and work experience. You might also include information about your career goal/objective, professional organizations you belong to, publications you read, and references. The rest of this chapter will explain how to organize and present all that information.

About You

List your full name, your address, and a phone number. If you live at school or if you are thinking of moving soon, include a permanent address as well as your current information. That way a potential employer can find you next week or in three months.

Do not include personal information in the resume. Because of equal employment laws, you will endanger your chances if you include information about your religion, marital status, race, or other personal details.

Education and Training

When listing your educational background, start with your most recent training and work backward. List your degree or certificate, the name and location of the school, and the date you graduated. Also include special programs or vendor training you have completed.

Computer Skills

Include names of software, hardware, networking protocols, and platforms you have worked with. Indicate your level of expertise (example: familiar with, experienced, expert).

Work Experience

List all computer-related experience, even if it isn't as a computer technician. Also list all customer service experience you have; every job requires customer service skills! Summer employment or part-time work should be labeled as such, and you will need to specify the months in the dates of employment for positions you held for less than a year.

If you just finished your training program, you might feel like you don't have much experience to list in a resume. Not true! Think back to those grueling school projects. Getting a grade on a project was only half the project's value. You can use it now in place of experience you have not yet gained in the workplace. List special projects with their title, a description, and lessons learned.

Other Information

Objective

Many resumes begin with a career goal or objective. It doesn't have to be profound or philosophical. Describe the job you want, the field in which you want to work, whether you want full- or part-time work, and whether you want employment or contract work. The purpose of the objective is to assure potential employers that they are about to read a relevant resume. The table below shows the relationship between a resume's objective and how the candidate will be viewed.

Position Title	Resume Objective	Good Candidate?
Software Support	Computer Technician	Yes
Technical Writer	Computer Technician	No
Desktop Technician	Computer Technician	Yes

Professional Organizations

If you belong to any professional organizations and read professional/trade publications, you can list them in a separate section of your resume.

References

Employers interested in hiring you may want to speak to people who can accurately (and favorably) represent your ability to do the job; these people are called references. Make a list of everyone you feel would be a good reference—those who would highly recommend you to an employer. However, don't include your family members; this list should be made up of former supervisors, teachers, or other adults you have worked or dealt with in the past and who know you well. Make sure you get permission from your references before listing them.

You can include references with each resume you send out, or you can simply state at the bottom of the resume that your references are available upon request. If you are responding to an advertisement, read it carefully to see if you are supposed to send references. If the ad does not mention them, you probably don't need to send them with your resume. List your references on a sheet of paper separate from your resume, but remember to include your name, address, and phone number on your reference list too.

How to Organize Your Resume

You can organize your resume in several ways. The most common types are:

- the chronological format
- the skills format (also known as a functional resume)
- a combination of chronological and skills format
- an electronically scannable format

The Chronological Resume

The most common resume format is chronological—you summarize your work experience year by year, beginning with your current or most recent employment experience and working backward. For each job, list the dates you were employed, the name and location of the company for which you worked, and the position(s) you held. See the sample chronological resume at the end of this chapter.

The Skills Resume

The skills resume (also known as the functional resume) emphasizes what you can do rather than what you have done. It is useful if you have large gaps in your work history or have relevant skills that would not be properly highlighted in a chronological listing of jobs. The skills resume concentrates on your skills and qualifications. Specific jobs you've held are listed, but they are not the primary focus of this type of resume. See the sample skills resume at the end of this chapter.

The Combination Resume

You may decide a combination of the chronological and skills resume would be best to highlight your skills. A combination resume allows for a mixture of your skills with a chronological list of jobs you've held. You get the best of both resumes. This is an excellent choice for students who have limited work experience and who want to highlight specific skills.

The Electronically Scannable Resume

At many large companies, all resumes from job applicants are scanned by a computer software program with optical character recognition (OCR) systems and entered into a database. Also, if you apply for jobs over the Internet via an email attachment, your resume requires special formatting so it can be read electronically. If your resume is going to be scanned electronically, it's best to:

- left-justify the entire document
- use Helvetica (a sans serif font) or Times or Courier font—size 10 to 14 points
- include a *keyword* section in which you list all keywords relevant to your job skills
- avoid tabs, symbols, boxes, graphics, and bullet points
- avoid italics, script, underlining, columns, or graphics
- use bold for emphasis
- avoid horizontal lines, parentheses, and brackets
- if sending a hard copy, print in crisp black ink on a laser printer and use high-quality white paper—do *not* send a fax or a photocopy

Resume Tips

- Always use standard letter-size ivory, cream, or neutral-color paper. A bright pink resume will stand out; it will also get laughed at and possibly thrown out.
- Include your name, address, and phone number on every page.
- Make sure your name is larger than anything else on the page (example: your name in 14-point font, the rest in 12 point).
- Use a font that is easy to read, such as 12-point Times New Roman.
- Do not use more than three fonts in your resume.

You **want** *it to* **look** like a **resume**, NOT a RANSOM note!

- Edit, edit, edit. Read it forward and backward. Have friends with good proofreading skills read it. Even if you have a grammar and spell checker on your computer, you still need to review it. For instance, a spell checker would not catch any of the errors in the following sentence: *Their are two many weighs too make errors that an computer does nut recognize.*
- Use bullet points for items in a list. If someone is glancing at your resume, it helps highlight the main points.
- Use key words in your industry.
- Avoid using excessive graphics such as boxes, distracting lines, and complex designs.

- Be consistent when using bold, capitalization, underlining, and italics. If one company name is underlined, make sure all are underlined. Also check titles and dates.

- Don't list your nationality, race, religion, or gender. Keep your resume as neutral as possible. Your resume is a summary of your skills and abilities.

- Don't put anything personal on your resume such as your birth date, marital status, height, or hobbies.

- One page is best, but do not crowd your resume. Shorten the margins if you need more space; if it's necessary to create a two-page resume, make sure you balance the information on each page. Don't put just one section on the second page. Be careful about where the page break occurs.

- Keep your resume updated. Don't write "9/97 to present" if you ended your job two months ago. Do not cross out or handwrite changes on your resume.

- Understand and remember everything written on your resume. Be able to back up all statements with specific examples.

Follow Up

Follow up each resume with a phone call. Wait one week after you mail the resume and then call the addressee to make sure it was received. You may even be able to set up an interview.

Resume Checklist

Use the following checklist when preparing your resume.

Task	Done
Include your name, address, and daytime phone number.	____
Include a career objective.	____
Include your educational background and any additional computer classes.	____
Include your work history, emphasizing anything related to computers.	____
Include a list of your computer software and hardware experience.	____
Include any memberships you have in professional organizations.	____
Check the resume for spelling and grammar errors.	____
Have someone else review your resume for errors before it is printed.	____
Print your resume in black ink on white, ivory, or neutral paper.	____

COVER LETTERS

The purpose of a cover letter is to provide the reader (your potential employer) with the following information at a glance:

- which job you are applying for
- where you heard about the opening
- an overview of your qualifications

Keep the cover letter short. The average hiring manager reads a cover letter for approximately three seconds, so you need to get the main point across in that time.

A hiring manager may have several similar job openings at one time, so you should clearly describe which job you are applying for. You can copy the title directly out of the advertisement; after all, the hiring manager probably wrote the ad and is very familiar with the terminology. Many human resources departments track the success of their ads, so name the source in which you saw the position advertised.

The cover letter is your opportunity to summarize your qualifications effectively. While it may be impressive to list all the details of all the jobs you have held, it's better to limit your cover letter to powerful statements such as "I have six years experience in the customer service industry and eight years experience repairing computers."

Address your cover letter to someone in particular, if possible. Take the time to do some investigating. Call the human resources department and ask for the name of the hiring manager or the human resources representative. If it is company policy not to give out names, at least get a formal title and use that in place of the name. Try to avoid simply using *Human Resources Representative* as a name. See the sample cover letter at the end of this chapter.

SUCCESSFUL INTERVIEWS

The only way to ace an interview is by being prepared. Showing that you understand the company's needs and can fulfill them will help you convince the interviewer that you are the right person for the job. Remember the guidelines listed below as you prepare for upcoming interviews.

Research the Company

Research the company before your interview and be ready to demonstrate your knowledge. Learn what the company does and try to read recent news releases to find out where it is planning to go in the future. You can research the company in many ways: look at its Internet Web site, read about it in industry magazines and newspapers, and talk to people who are familiar with it. At a minimum, you should know the size of the company, what it does, and its main products or services.

Act Professional

Take the interviewing process very seriously. You are entering the professional world, and you want to show that you will fit into that environment. It is important to be on time for your interview. Allow extra time for traffic and getting lost if the interview is in an unfamiliar location. Schedule your travel time so that you are in the lobby 10 minutes before your interview starts. This will give you time to relax before you start the interview.

Although your interview is not a fashion show, take the time to dress properly. Depending on the culture of the company, proper attire could be anything from a suit to khakis. Make sure that your clothes are free of stains and wrinkles. And if you must make a choice, it is better to be overdressed than underdressed. A desktop technician supervisor offers this warning:

> I interviewed nine candidates for a desktop technician position recently. Of the seven men I interviewed, four of them came to the interview in casual clothes. I thought that was very inappropriate; they didn't have to wear suits, but they should have at least worn ties. They probably won't wear ties in their daily jobs, but everyone should dress well for an interview.

Speak Confidently

Greet your interviewer with a firm handshake and an enthusiastic smile. Speak with confidence throughout your interview and address your comments as if you assume you will be getting the job. For example, phrase your questions this way: "What would my typical day consist of?" "How many people would be on my team, and what are their areas of expertise?" Answer questions in complete sentences, not just *yes* or *no*. However, don't ramble on too long answering any one question; try limiting your answers to under two minutes each. Many hiring managers will ask questions that don't have a right or wrong answer; they ask such questions to evaluate your problem-solving skills. The following table contains the most common interview questions and some tips on how to answer them.

Question	Answer Tip
Tell me about yourself.	Do not provide any personal information (marital status, kids, religion, hobbies). Only give information about your training, computer experience, and work experience. Practice answering this question before you go on an interview; it can be disarming if you're not ready for it.
What are your strengths and weaknesses?	Be honest. They want to know because they are evaluating not only your skills and education but how well you will fit in to the work environment. If you aren't honest, it will show up eventually. Emphasize your strengths more than your weaknesses and mention only weaknesses that won't break the company!
What do you know about our company?	This is the opportunity to impress the hiring manager by showing that you had the initiative and drive to research the company before you interviewed. Make sure you have something positive to say.
Why should we hire you?	Draw from the information you already discussed concerning your strengths and how your strengths can fill their needs.

Ask Questions

You usually will be given the opportunity to ask the interviewer questions, so be prepared. Have a list of questions ready in advance. There's much you need to know about the company and the hiring manager to determine if the company is a good fit for you. It's not just a one-way street—while you are being evaluated, you are also evaluating the company to see if it's a working environment you want. If you don't ask any questions, the hiring manager may think that you aren't interested in the position. Here are some examples of the types of questions you might want to ask in an interview:

* What would my typical day consist of?
* What would my level of responsibility be?
* What are the work hours?
* What is your management style? (directed to the interviewer)
* What is the possibility for promotion in the next two years?

Know the Interview Format

Large companies usually expect formal attire and hold formal interviews. You probably will have to interview with two to five people and may be required to come back for two or three rounds of interviews. The longer the hiring process takes, the less likely the company is to lay off its staff. It takes great pains to hire only as many people as are needed and only those who will grow with the company.

Smaller companies are the largest employers right now. They are hiring more people more quickly than any other employer. The smaller companies usually require that you undergo only one or two interviews for a job. Your first interview generally will be with the person who will make the final decision in this stream-lined process.

Universities generally require that computer personnel fill out a qualifications form along with the job application as a screening process. If your qualifications don't measure up, you won't get an interview. If you pass the qualifications portion of the application, you will be contacted for an interview and probably will have at least two interviews.

Government agencies test applicants to make sure they meet the job requirements. They have regularly scheduled exam dates and will keep the results on hand, so you can refer to them if you find a job you'd like to apply for. Contact your local state or city government to find out the testing dates; you also can purchase a set of booklets called *The Federal Job Winner's Tips*, published by the federal government to help job seekers obtain government jobs.

Follow Up

After the interview, follow up with a thank-you note, email, or voice mail message to the interviewer. Following up lets interviewers know that you are serious about the position and also helps them remember you better. Here are some tips for following up:

* Have plenty of notepaper and stamps available. A thank-you note is most effective when it is written on the same day as your interview and mailed right away.
* Send a separate note to each person you interviewed with, and make each one personal. Refer to something that happened during the interview, such as a tour of the building or the introductions to the present job holder.
* Check your note for spelling and grammar errors. You are trying to reinforce the impression that you are the right candidate.

Chronological Resume Sample

Christine McDonald
5110 Appleview Road
Watertown, ND 50298
703-425-7322

Objective

To obtain a contract position as a computer technician.

Work Experience

November 1997–present
Brown Publishing Company, Watertown, ND
Hardware and Software Technician
Performed software rollout of Microsoft Office to 300 employees. Installed and supported Microsoft applications, hardware and software; helped users with hardware and software problems.

June 1995–November 1997
Torrance Supplies, Watertown, ND
Hardware and Software Technician / Help Desk / Network Technician
Hardware and software installation, helped users with hardware and software problems, repaired Banyan and Windows NT 4.0 problems on contract to Texaco E & P.

April 1993–June 1995
Ace Advertising, Watertown, ND
Graphic Artist
Handled large volume of ad design, pasteup, and layout for newsletters.
Took on extra duties and became heavily involved in desktop maintenance and troubleshooting.

October 1992–April 1993
Crown Travel, Inc., Watertown, ND
Customer Service Agent / Manager on Duty
Consistently scored high on monitored calls providing customer assistance in a call center. Promoted to Manager on Duty within two months, serving as first line of technical support to customers.

Education

Associate of Science, Midtown College, Watertown, ND, 1992

Microsoft Certified System Engineer, 1995

A+ Certification, 1997

Skills

Experienced with Windows 95, Windows 3.1 & 3.11, MS Office 95 & 97, Harvard Graphics, WordPerfect, and Corel Draw.

Familiar with Novell NetWare 3.12, Banyan Vines, MS FrontPage, and Doc-to-Help.

References available upon request.

Skills Resume Sample

Kevin Singh
5110 Viewcrest Road
Mesa, AZ 11223
948-230-3843

Objective

A position as a computer technician.

Qualifications

♦ Proficient in all Windows and Macintosh platforms.

♦ Proficient in TCP/IP, NetBeui, and IPX networking protocols.

♦ Proficient with most office and publishing applications including: Excel, Word, WordPerfect, PageMaker, and Photoshop.

♦ Expert in hardware and software installation.

♦ Expert in basic hardware maintenance and repair.

Professional Experience

♦ Assisted students with desktop needs and provided troubleshooting for student computer lab.

♦ Developed online cataloging system for instructor materials.

♦ Involved in the maintenance and expansion of campus-wide network.

♦ Assisted in the maintenance of over 1500 computers and data terminals utilizing a wide variety of operating systems including Windows, Macintosh, and Unix.

♦ Advised customers on what hardware and software to buy to fit their needs.

♦ Performed small upgrades in shop on desktops and notebooks.

Employment History

Computer Lab Technician, **Mesa College–Mesa, AZ,** June 1995– present

Computer Sales, **Office Supplies Unlimited–Mesa, AZ,** February 1993–June 1995

Computer Sales and Upgrades, **Office Supplies Unlimited, Mesa, AZ,** August 1992–February 1993

Education

Associate degree in computer science, 1997

Pleasant Community College

Mesa, AZ 11226

References available upon request.

Sample Cover Letter

Jana Polowski
38320 Highway 66
Atlanta, GA 80293

January 31, 1998

Corrine Michaels
Human Resources Manager
Medical Devices Company
99302 Oak Street
Naples, GA 90233

Dear Ms. Michaels:

Please accept my resume for the desktop computer technician position advertised in the *Tribune* on Sunday, January 30.

As required, I have a two-year computer science degree and am certified through Microsoft. I have six years of experience in the customer service industry and eight years of experience servicing computers.

I am available for an interview immediately and available to begin work two weeks after I am hired. I look forward to meeting you in the interview.

Regards,

Jana Polowski

Enclosure: resume

Who:	Nancy Lee
What:	Software support technician
Where:	Indiana
How much:	$34,000 per year

Insider's Advice

I advise you to decide which aspects of computing you enjoy most and pursue a very thorough knowledge of that field; however, the more you can learn about the other aspects of computer technology, the more valuable you'll be to a potential employer.

The field of computer technology is changing daily, and that means you must continue learning and monitoring each new advancement. Shop around to find training courses. You might even find places that will offer you a package deal for multiple programs. Read manuals on specific applications and equipment. Consider joining a professional organization or a software users' group in your interest and area. These groups will be a valuable source of information and technical knowledge.

And last but not least, network as much as possible to improve your contacts. An employer contacted through networking is likely to look more closely at your ability than your educational level. Professional organizations and user groups can be a wonderful source for networking. Training classes are also good places to meet people who might be in a position to help, especially the trainers. Conferences and seminars are another important source for networking, and they keep you current on both lingo and applications.

Insider's Take on the Future

I am planning to apply for a job in the network support area of my company. I sit next to the network technicians, and they seem to be on the run all the time. It seems that every day they have some new problem that nobody knows how to solve. I think that would be fun—kind of like being a detective. I know so much about the software we use that I can learn any new upgrades to that software in a matter of minutes; I am anxious to move into something new.

CHAPTER | 6

This chapter will show you how to survive and thrive in your new career. You'll find out how to manage work relationships, fit into the workplace culture, manage your time, find a mentor, and make your mark at work.

HOW TO SUCCEED ONCE YOU'VE LANDED THE JOB

Landing the job is one thing. Succeeding at the job is another. After investing your time and money to complete a training program and land a job, you'll want to arm yourself with as much information as possible to succeed as a computer technician.

MANAGING WORK RELATIONSHIPS
Basic Rules
Some basic rules apply to any workplace. If you're aware of them, they can help get you out of a bind or even prevent you from getting into one.

1. **Sometimes peace is better than justice.**

    You may be right about a situation. You may be sure you are right. Unfortunately, you may have coworkers who doubt you or who flatly disagree with you. In some situations, you need to assert your position and convince the disbelievers to trust your judgment. However, carefully consider the gravity of the situation before you stick your neck out. In other words, pick your fights wisely. For instance, go ahead and argue your position if you can prevent a catastrophe such as a computer crash or a network failure. On the other hand, if you are having a debate about an issue of taste, opinion, or preference, you may want to leave the situation alone. Let your recommendation be known, but do not argue your point relentlessly. Sometimes you will be right and people will not listen to you. That's life; it will happen. Settle for peace to save a work relationship or to save time.

2. **Don't burn any bridges.**

If you are in a disagreement, or if you are leaving one position for another, or if a project is ending, always leave the work relationship on a good note. Don't take the opportunity to speak your mind in a ranting and raving manner before you leave. While it might make you feel good for about three minutes, it will have a lasting effect on your career and on people's perception of you. Someone you told off could become your boss someday or might be able to help you down the line. Even if you don't ever have contact with that person again, he or she will have contact with many other people and possibly describe you as hard to work with or downright rude. Your work reputation is very important; don't tarnish it by burning your bridges.

3. **Keep work and social life separate.**

You were hired to do a job, not to meet new friends and potential dates. While it's important to be friendly and form positive relationships with the people you work with, beware of becoming too chummy. Personal relationships can wreak havoc in the workplace. Consider that you might have to rate a friend's job performance, take work direction from a buddy, or fire someone you hang out with. Some people even become romantically involved with people at work. There are many reasons not to do so: seeing your heartthrob around the office distracts you from your work; romantic relationships spark rumors; breakups are hard enough without seeing your ex in the office every day; and so on. It is wise to keep your work relationships professional.

Managing Relationships with Your Customers

As a computer technician, you will be working in customer service. Unfortunately, your customers are often panicked when they need you. When people call a computer technician, it is usually because something is wrong with their computer or network. They are upset, they are getting behind in their work, they are frustrated, and they may be crabby. Don't take their frustration personally; it's not about you. It's about the job they can't get done until you have done yours.

As a customer service expert, you need to be empathetic. Try a little humor, a gentle smile, and assurance that you will solve the problem as quickly as you can.

Managing Relationships with Your Coworkers

You will meet many people in the course of your career. Some you will admire; some you will find barely tolerable. For your personal development, you need to find a way to work well with all of them.

Many companies have internal training departments or allow their employees to take external business classes and seminars. Either way, take advantage of every opportunity you have to enroll in courses or workshops about human relations, conflict resolution, and personal development. They will help you learn more about your personal style and how to work more effectively with a variety of other personalities. Courses about positive conflict resolution can be especially helpful if you work with highly confrontational people. Taking such courses can help make you better at customer service and increase your potential for moving into management positions.

Here are a couple of fundamental rules for fostering positive working relationships with your peers:

- Don't gossip about your boss, your coworkers, or anyone else. Gossip hurts the person being talked about, will inevitably come back to haunt you, and also can make you look like you don't have enough to do!
- Foster sharing relationships instead of competitive relationships. If you experiment with a great new piece of software or read an interesting article in a computer magazine, share the information with your coworkers. A group of people who help each other develop professionally will shine as a team and as individuals. On the other hand, if you jockey for position and compete over everything, you will miss out on the wealth that you could learn from your coworkers (and will have to live in a strained work environment).

Managing Your Relationship with Your Boss

Depending on your boss, this relationship can be pleasurable or painful. In any case, it's important to keep the communication lines open. Talk to your boss about his or her management style and adjust your expectations to work within that style. For instance, your boss might like to be hands-on and help you troubleshoot problems. She might want to talk to you at least once a day to hear about your activities. You need to understand that this boss wants to empower you through a mentoring/teaching style. On the other hand, your boss might want you to call him only if you have a problem and simply submit a weekly status report on your projects. You need to understand that this boss wants to empower you through a hands-off style that lets you find your own solutions. Both bosses may be good managers; they simply have different styles. Understand the value of each style and get the most from it.

Also talk to your boss about your career goals. Set goals for six months, one year, three years, and five years. Based on your discussions, you and your boss can create projects and strategies to lead you toward your goals. If you are a people person and an organizer, you might want to move toward a management position and set relevant goals. If you love the hands-on, rapidly changing technical environment, you might choose to specialize in one type of technical work or move toward another area such as database administrator or programmer. No matter what you are interested in, make a plan, share it with your boss, and get a few steps closer to achieving your goals.

Fitting into the Workplace Culture

Workplace cultures can vary widely, from formal and stiff to relaxed and casual. The three main types are entrepreneurial, small business, and corporate.

An entrepreneurial culture emphasizes risk-taking and working independently. Entrepreneurial cultures often admire and reward a well-presented (flashy and stylish) idea. You are selling your idea, and the sale takes some pizzazz. Entrepreneurial cultures often are competitive; they are frequently in quick, big-money fields and often pay on commission. The advantage of entrepreneurial cultures, of course, is that they often pay well. The disadvantage is the overly competitive and stressful atmosphere.

Despite the name, small business cultures are not always found in small companies. While entrepreneurial cultures are competitive, small business cultures are more relaxed and informal. They often nurture as many new ideas as any other type of workplace, but they don't have such a competitive edge. The team culture is more of a cooperative, brainstorming, *think tank* environment. If one person is successful, everyone shares the success. The advantage of this type of culture is that it fosters a pleasant working environment that promotes growth and cooperation. The disadvantage is that jobs in this environment often do not pay as much as in other cultures.

The third workplace culture is corporate. This culture relies on a reporting structure and hierarchy to accomplish defined goals. Many large companies adopt this style simply because they have a large number of people to deal with. One manager (or president or vice president) cannot talk to everyone in the company all the time about their ideas. Instead, there's a functional reporting system. You might have a president, who has seven vice presidents, who has seven directors, who has seven managers, one of whom has you and several coworkers in his or her reporting chain. For employees, the advantage in this type of culture is usually security—job security, the availability of additional training (often company paid), and a good, long-term salary. The disadvantage is that employees do not have as much freedom as in other cultures and may have to spend more time writing reports and filling out forms than do those in other workplace cultures.

There is no perfect workplace culture. You need to find one that suits your needs. Do you want financial security and continued training? Then go for a large corporate environment. Are you willing to put in a lot of hours for quick money? Then pursue an entrepreneurial culture. Are you searching for a cooperative, stable working environment? Then a small company is probably right for you.

You may think you would not fit into certain cultures, but try not to discount anything out of hand. Decide which you think will be the best fit and try it; but remain willing to try another culture if a great opportunity arises.

MANAGING YOUR TIME

You'll most likely find that the workplace environment is more hectic than school was, so you will need to manage your time effectively to make the most of your workweek. Here are some tips for juggling your tasks and managing your time.

Daily Work Activities

1. **Know the requirements of your job and what your boss expects of you.**
   Define your role and know what you are expected to deliver on a daily
   basis.

   ◆ Customer service—Are you supposed to be available for customer service
   at a moment's notice? If so, ensure that you are not overloaded with other
   tasks that will get in the way of customer service. Do not agree to get
   projects done by a certain deadline if you're on call; you never know when
   your customers will need you. Use time between customer service calls to
   learn new software, catch up on projects that aren't time-sensitive, or read
   computer-related publications.

   ◆ Defined deliverables—Are you given a defined set of tasks to accomplish
   within a defined period of time? If you are at this end of the spectrum,
   don't let yourself get distracted from your tasks. Make a task list or "to do"
   list using a calendar. Estimate what you need to be doing every hour of the
   day to accomplish your tasks and then stick as close as possible to your
   schedule.

   ◆ Combination—Are you somewhere between the two, given a defined set
   of tasks to accomplish whenever you have time but expected to be available for customer service? If so, negotiate target deadlines with your boss
   so the tasks don't drag on forever, but make customer service your top
   priority. If the deadline looks impossible to meet, see if you can get an
   extension before it comes. Use down time between service calls to accomplish the activities on your task list.

2. **Don't get trapped by interruptions and time wasters.** Every job is subject
   to time wasters. Sometimes you may get caught up by people who want to
   chat socially; or you may fall into the trap of playing computer games or
   reading the news. It is important to allow yourself a small amount of relax-
   ation throughout the day, but set limits for yourself—such as 15 minutes
   per day—so it doesn't get out of control. If you work with a social, chatty
   person, don't let yourself be distracted or interrupted. If you are working
   on something, let your coworker know that you are busy and can perhaps
   talk later, during lunch. If you do have time to talk to your coworker, try
   to steer the conversation to computer-related topics. Use the time to learn
   something new from your coworker rather than just chat.

3. **Keep a day planner.** Identify one place where you write everything down, whether it is a formal day planner or a spiral notebook. It is best to separate the space into categories: a calendar, tasks, notes from meetings, things to remember, and contacts (names and phone numbers). It is most efficient to use a formal day planner, which is designed for exactly that use. Some people like to use a book they can carry; others prefer an online day planner. Either way, it can really help you organize yourself.

Managing Life and a Job

When you are at work every day all week long, it becomes difficult to get your *life tasks* done. Here are some tips to help you integrate your job with your life.

- Make lists. Keep a list of things you need to do, buy, return, pick up, and drop off. A day planner is the best place to keep such a list. If you don't have a day planner, carry a notebook with you from home to work and back again. Organize your list according to places you will stop. Keep grocery items on one list, pharmacy items on another, dry cleaning on a third, and so on. Cross things off the lists when you have finished them so you can see what you have to do at a glance.
- Use your lunch hour to run errands at least once a week. Identify resources that are close to your work for things you can do during your lunch hour—doctor, dentist, dry cleaner, shoe repair, car repair, hardware store, and so on.
- Use the commute between home and work to take care of other errands, such as stopping at daycare and the grocery store.

FINDING A MENTOR

A mentor is someone you identify as successful and with whom you create a teacher-student relationship. Choose your mentor based on what is important to you and on how you define success. Someone can be successful without having attained certain titles or positions, so keep an open mind when you're looking for a mentor. A mentor is someone you can learn from. Enter into the relationship intending to observe your mentor carefully and ask many questions.

There are two primary types of mentors: a business mentor and a technical mentor. You will learn different things from each type of mentor. A business mentor will provide guidance about how to be successful in the business culture.

Although each mentoring situation is different, you often can learn the following from a business mentor:

- customer service skills
- presentation skills
- how to design a career plan
- how to set incremental goals
- what to expect in your business culture
- how to communicate with your boss
- how to gain sponsorship for your ideas

A technical mentor, on the other hand, is someone who has more technical knowledge than you do and can teach you those skills, direct your path for ongoing learning, and help you develop technical problem-solving skills. You often can learn the following from a technical mentor:

- problem-solving skills
- in-depth knowledge about technology used by your company
- tricks and shortcuts for repair and maintenance
- trends in technology
- which computer magazines are best
- which conferences/seminars/classes you should attend

How to Connect With a Mentor

Don't just wait for your fairy godmother to appear and provide you with a mentor; actively search for one! A mentor can be anyone from a senior-level manager to one of your peers. Remember, finding a good mentor is not a matter of title, years in the business, or years with your company. A good mentor is someone who is expert in a certain area and willing and able to teach you.

There are many ways to find a mentor. Since you probably will be looking for a mentor when you start your new job, you won't know many people at the company. Try these techniques for identifying possible mentors:

- Ask your boss to recommend someone. Let your supervisor know that you are proactively trying to improve yourself through a mentor. This actually helps you in two ways. First, it helps you find an appropriate mentor based on your boss's experience at the company and in the industry. Second, it lets your boss know that you are serious about your career and your personal development.

◆ Observe people. You can learn a lot this way. When asked a question, do they take the time to help you find a resolution or do they point you toward someone else who can help you? The one who takes the time to help you resolve your question is the better choice for a mentor. How does the potential mentor resolve problems? In a calm manner? Do problems get resolved? If so, you've found a good candidate.

◆ Listen to people who admire your potential mentor. What qualities do they admire? Do the admirable qualities coincide with your values and goals? If you need to learn conflict-resolution skills, you probably shouldn't consider a mentor who is admired for a forceful, aggressive style. Instead, look for someone people describe as fair, calm, and easy to work with.

PROMOTING YOURSELF

Once you have a job, you can promote yourself in many ways. No, you can't give yourself a raise or a better job title, but you can position yourself for success. An excellent way to do that is by setting realistic, tangible career goals. This shows that you take your job seriously and that you expect promotion. However, it's not enough to set goals and keep them to yourself. You need to share your goals with your managers, so they know when you have achieved each goal; then they can reward you. Make an appointment to discuss your goals with your boss, and remember to be open to your boss's ideas for possible goals. Goals can be specific tasks you want to accomplish or personality characteristics you want to improve. For example, to finish a comprehensive report about computer maintenance trends, or deal with difficult people better. You also can discuss your goals with a human resources representative so your name will come to mind when a suitable job opens up. Expand your contacts on the job and share your successes with them to build a strong position for future growth.

THE INSIDE TRACK

Who:	Marcio Ramirez
What:	Desktop technician
Where:	Washington, D.C.
How much:	$28,000 per year

Insider Advice

I got my degree in accounting and had a job in an accounting firm for a few years. I was the guy everyone called on to help with their computers. I experimented with computers and read a lot and eventually was considered the computer expert in my office. I decided I was more interested in computers than in accounting, so I took a job as a computer technician based on my experience. My advice to anyone entering the technician field is to take every opportunity to get hands-on experience.

Insider's Take on the Future

I plan to become certified through Novell and Microsoft because my peers will have a competitive advantage over me if they are certified and I'm not. As my company does, I think that more and more businesses will choose to invest in a single product manufacturer, such as Microsoft or Lotus, for all of their software, because it is too hard to maintain products by multiple vendors with multiple products and multiple releases.

APPENDIX A

PROFESSIONAL ASSOCIATIONS

This appendix includes a list of computer-related associations. By joining these associations, you become eligible for member benefits that each organization has to offer. You'll also find a list of accrediting associations, which you should contact before you enroll in a school to make sure it's accredited.

Here is a list of professional associations for computer technicians. You may want to contact one or more of these associations for information on all facets of the computer technician profession.

COMPUTER-RELATED ASSOCIATIONS

National Computer Security Association (NCSA)

NCSA is an independent organization that promotes continuous improvement of commercial digital security through the application of the NCSA Risk Framework and NCSA Continuous Certification Model to certification, research, and related activities. NCSA's goal is to improve global security, trust, and confidence in computing through the certification of products, systems, and people.

Benefits
Membership benefits include:

- *NCSA News*
- anti-virus support
- discounts

Contact Information

http://www.ncsa.com
717-241-3250

Association for Computing Machinery (ACM)

ACM, founded in 1947, is an international scientific and educational organization dedicated to advancing the art, science, engineering, and application of information technology. It promotes an exchange of information and promotes high professional and ethical standards.

Benefits

Membership benefits include:

- a year's subscription to *Communications of the ACM* (12 issues)
- access to CareerLine, a free email service
- discounts

Contact Information

acmhelp@acm.org
212-626-0500

Association for Women in Computing (AWC)

AWC is a not-for-profit, professional organization for individuals with an interest in information technology. AWC is dedicated to the advancement of women in the computing fields, in business, industry, science, education, government, and technology.

Benefits

Membership benefits include:

- monthly meetings with guest speakers, panel discussions, and workshops
- technical and motivational seminars
- job listings and career planning
- scholarships
- skill enhancement

Contact Information

http://www.awc-hq.org

Association for Women in Computing

Independent Membership Application

41 Sutter St., Suite 1006

San Francisco, CA 94104

USENIX

USENIX is the Advanced Computing Systems Association. Since 1975 the USENIX Association has brought together the community of engineers, system administrators, scientists, and technicians working in the computing world.

Benefits

Membership benefits include:

* optional membership in SAGE, the System Administrators Guild
* free subscription to the association magazine
* access to papers from the USENIX conferences and symposia
* discounts

Contact Information

http://www.usenix.org

510-528-8649

The USENIX Association

2560 Ninth St., Suite 215

Berkeley, CA 94710

Computer Professionals for Social Responsibility (CPSR)

CPSR is a public-interest alliance of computer scientists and others concerned about the impact of computer technology on society. They work to influence decisions regarding the development and use of computers. As technical experts, CPSR members provide the public and policymakers with realistic assessments of the power, promise, and limitations of computer technology.

Benefits

Membership benefits include:

* opportunity to affect policymaking at the local, regional, and national level
* a quarterly newsletter
* discounts

Contact Information

http://www.cpsr.org/dox/home.html

CPSR

P.O. Box 717

Palo Alto, CA 94302

IEEE Computer Society

The IEEE Computer Society is an organization of computer professionals. The society promotes an active exchange of information, ideas, and technological innovation among its members. Professionals may join the IEEE Computer Society alone or in conjunction with the IEEE.

Benefits

Membership benefits include:

- *Computer* magazine, a publication of the IEEE Computer Society
- opportunities to enhance individual professional development through local and student chapter meetings and activities
- easy access to books and proceedings produced by the Computer Society Press

Contact Information

Members may join the Computer Society by itself, or in conjunction with joining the IEEE.

http://www.computer.org

714-821-8380

IEEE Computer Society

Attn: Membership

10662 Los Vaqueros Circle

P.O. Box 3014

Los Alamitos, CA 90720-1314

The Institute of Electrical and Electronics Engineers (IEEE)

IEEE is a technical professional society. Founded in 1884 by a handful of practitioners of the new electrical engineering discipline, today the IEEE includes more than 320,000 members who conduct and participate in its activities in 147 countries.

IEEE membership is open to professionals with varying amounts of education and work experience. Member, Senior Member, and Fellow grades are limited to those who have achieved professional competence and recognition, as demonstrated by their degrees and their work experience. Associate grade is open to certain technical and non-technical applicants who may benefit from membership and participation in the IEEE, and also to those progressing through education and work experience toward Member grade.

Benefits

Membership benefits include:

- technical conferences, symposia, and meetings
- educational programs

Contact Information

http://www.ieee.org
800-678-IEEE(4333)
IEEE Operations Center
Admission and Advancement Department
445 Hoes Ln., P.O. Box 459
Piscataway, NJ 08855-0459

Internet Society

The Internet Society is a non-governmental international organization for global cooperation and coordination for the Internet and its internetworking technologies and applications.

Benefits

Membership benefits include:

- conferences
- education and training
- publications
- discounts

Contact Information

http://www.isoc.org/membership
FAX: 703-648-9887

Association of Information Technology Professionals (AITP)

The AITP offers its members opportunities for professional and personal growth, helping them to achieve career objectives and meet the challenges of the Information Systems profession.

Benefits

Membership benefits include:

- computer forms and supplies
- employment services
- financial services
- group insurance plans
- LAN CBT training
- magazine subscriptions
- discounts

Contact Information

70430.35@compuserve.com
800-224-9371 x242
AITP
505 Busse Hwy.
Park Ridge, IL 60068

Network Professional Association (NPA)

The NPA is a non-profit organization for networking professionals who design, implement, and maintain computer networks. The NPA's mission is to advance the network computing profession by educating and providing resources for its members. The NPA accepts and encourages multi-vendor certification and education on the part of its nearly 7,000 members in 100 chapters worldwide.

Benefits

Membership benefits include:

- free software
- *Network Professional Journal* (NPJ)
- CNP (Certified Network Professional Program)
- discounts

Contact Information

http://www.npa.org/about/membership.htm
888-379-0910
Network Professional Association
401 N. Michigan Ave.
Chicago, IL 60611-4255

ACCREDITING ASSOCIATIONS

Here is a list of national and regional accrediting agencies for you to contact to see if your chosen school is accredited. You can request a list of schools that each agency accredits.

National Accrediting Agencies

Accrediting Council for Independent Colleges and Schools (ACICS)

750 First St. NE, Suite 980
Washington, DC 20002-4242
202-336-6780; FAX: 202-842-2593

Accrediting Commission of Career Schools and Colleges of Technology

750 First St. NE, Suite 905
Washington, DC 20002-4242
202-336-6850; FAX: 202-842-2585

Accrediting Commission of Distance Education and Training Council

1601 18th St., NW
Washington, DC 20009-2529
202-234-5100; FAX: 202-332-1386

National Association of Trade and Technical Schools (NATTS)

2251 Wisconsin Ave., NW
Washington, DC 20009
202-333-1021

National Home Study Council (NHSC)

1601 Eighteenth St. NW
Washington, DC 20009
202-234-5100

Computing Sciences Accreditation Board (CSAB)

Suite 209, Two Landmark Square
Stamford, CT 06901
203-975-1117; FAX: 203-975-1222

Regional Accreditation Agencies

Middle States Association of Colleges and Schools (MSACS)
3624 Market St.
Philadelphia, PA 19104-2680
215-662-5606; FAX: 215-662-5501

New England Association of Schools and Colleges (NEASC)
209 Burlington Rd.
Bedford, MA 01730-1433
617-271-0022; FAX: 617-271-0950

North Central Association of Colleges and Schools (NCACS)
159 North Dearborn St.
Chicago, IL 60601
312-263-0456; FAX: 312-263-7462

Northwest Association of Schools and Colleges (NASC)
Boise State University
1910 University Dr.
Boise, ID 83725
208-334-3226; FAX: 208-334-3228

Southern Association of Colleges and Schools (SACS)
1866 Southern Ln.
Decatur, GA 30033-4097
404-679-4500; FAX: 404-679-4558

Western Association of Schools and Colleges (WASC)
533 Airport Blvd., Suite 200
Burlingame, CA 94010
415-375-7711; FAX: 415-375-7790

Accrediting Agency Responsible for Each State

State	Regional Accrediting Agency	State	Regional Accrediting Agency
Alabama	SACS	Nebraska	NCACS
Alaska	NASs	Nevada	NASC
American Samoa	WASC	New Hampshire	NEASC
Arizona	NCACS	New Jersey	MSACS
Arkansas	NCACS	New Mexico	NCACS
California	WASC	New York	MSACS
Colorado	NCACS	North Carolina	SACS
Connecticut	NEASC	North Dakota	NCACS
Delaware	MSACS	Northern Marianas	WASC
District of Columbia	MSACS	Ohio	NCACS
Florida	SACS	Oklahoma	NCACS
Georgia	SACS	Oregon	NASC
Guam	WASC	Pacific Islands	WASC
Hawaii	WASC	Pennsylvania	MSACS
Idaho	NASC	Puerto Rico	MSACS
Illinois	NCACS	Republic of Panama	MSACS
Indiana	NCACS	Rhode Island	NEASC
Iowa	NCACS	South Dakota	NCACS
Kansas	NCACS	Tennessee	SACS
Kentucky	SACS	Texas	SACS
Louisiana	SACS	U.S. Virgin Islands	MSACS
Maine	NEASC	Utah	NASC
Maryland	MSACS	Vermont	NEASC
Massachusetts	NEASC	Virginia	SACS
Michigan	NCACS	Washington	NASC
Minnesota	NCACS	West Virginia	NCACS
Mississippi	SACS	Wisconsin	NCACS
Missouri	NCACS	Wyoming	NCACS
Montana	NASC		

APPENDIX B

After you've been through this entire book and have a good idea of what steps you need to take to accomplish your goals, look through this appendix for titles that will give you more specific advice on areas you need help in.

ADDITIONAL RESOURCES

For additional information on the topics discussed in this book, refer to the following reading list of books organized by subject and the extensive list of computer-related magazines and web addresses that follows.

Books

Finding the Right College

Occupational Outlook Handbook. U.S. Department of Labor. 1996.

The College Blue Book. Macmillan Library Reference. 1997.

Peterson's Guide to Colleges for Careers in Computing. Princeton, NJ: Peterson's Guides. 1996.

Peterson's Guide to Two-Year Colleges 1998: The Only Guide to More than 1,500 Community and Junior Colleges. Princeton, NJ: Peterson's. 1997.

Finding Certification

Gilius, Lawrence. *The Complete Guide to Certification for Computing Professionals.* New York: Computing McGraw-Hill. 1995.

Gatlin, Anthony J. and John Paul Mueller. *The Complete Microsoft Certification Success Guide.* New York: Computing McGraw-Hill. 1997.

Williams, Robert and John P. Mueller. *The Novell Certification Handbook.* New York: Computing McGraw-Hill. 1996.

Parks, Sarah T. and Bob Kalman. *The A+ Certification Success Guide for Computer Technicians.* New York: Computing McGraw-Hill. 1996.

Related Computer Careers

Eberts, Marjorie and Margaret Gisler. *Careers for Computer Buffs and Other Technological Types.* Chicago: VGM Career Horizons. 1993.

Weintraub, Joseph. *Exploring Careers in the Computer Field.* Rosen Publishing Group. 1987.

Burns, Julie Kling. *Opportunities in Computer Science Careers.* Chicago: VGM Career Horizons. 1996.

Southworth, Scott. *Exploring High Tech Careers.* Rosen Publishing Group. 1993.

Career and Job Hunting Guidance

Riley, Margaret and Frances Roehm, Steve Oserman and the Public Library Association. *Guide to Internet Job Searching.* Chicago: VGM Career Horizons. 1996.

Williams, Marcia P. and Sue A. Cubbage. *The 1997 National Job Hotline Directory.* New York: McGraw-Hill. 1997.

Krantz, Les. *The World Almanac Job Finder's Guide 1997.* St. Martin's Press. 1996.

Yate, Martin John. *Knock 'em Dead with Great Answers to Tough Interview Questions.* Adams Publishing. 1985.

Bolles, Richard Nelson. *What Color is your Parachute?* Ten Speed Press. 1997.

Adams Media Corporation. *Adams Jobs Almanac.* Adams Publishing. 1997.

Krannich, Caryl Rae and Ronald L. Krannich.. *101 Dynamite Answers to Interview Questions: Sell your Strengths!* Impact Publications. 1997

Fein, Richard. *101 Dynamite Questions to Ask at your Job Interview.* Impact Publications. 1996.

Rothstein, Michael. *Ace the Technical Interview.* New York: Computing McGraw-Hill. 1996.

Farr, Michael. *America's Top Jobs for People without College Degrees.* Jist Works. 1996.

Magazines

Here are the names of several computer-related magazines and their web addresses to help you keep up to date with current and emerging computer technology trends.

Publication Title	URL
BYTE	http://www.byte.com
CIO magazine	http://www.cio.com/CIO
ClieNT Server News	http://www.computerwire.com/csnews/
Cobb Group	http://www.cobb.com/
CommunicationsWeek	http://techweb.cmp.com/techweb/cw/current/default.html
Communications Technology	http://www.ctinfosite.com/
Computer Currents	http://www.currents.net/
Computer Life	http://www.complife.ziff.com/~complife/
Computer Shopper	http://www5.zdnet.com/cshopper/
Computerworld	http://careers.computerworld.com/cwnews/subform.html
Crossroads:The International ACM Student Magazine	http://info.acm.org/crossroads/
Home Computing and Entertainment	http://www.plesman.com/hce/
Home PC	http://techweb.cmp.com/techweb/hpc/current/default.html
HotWired Online Magazine	http://www.wired.com/
InformationWeek	http://techweb.cmp.com/techweb/iw/current/default.html
InfoWorld	http://www.infoworld.com/
Internet Business Report	http://www.jup.com/newsletter/business/
Internet Week	http://www.phillips.com/iw/

Publication Title	URL
Internet World	http://www.internetworld.com/
LAN Magazine	http://www.lanmag.com/
LAN Product News	http://www.newsnet.com/libiss/ec99.html
Microsoft Magazine	http://www.microsoft.com/magazine/
Microsoft Systems Journal	http://www.msj.com/
NetGuide	http://techweb.cmp.com/techweb/ntg/current/default.html
Network Computing	http://techweb.cmp.com/techweb/nc/current/default.html
PC Computing	http://www.zdnet.com/pccomp/
PC Digest	http://www.nstl.com/pcd.htm
PC Week	http://www.pcweek.com/
PC World	http://www.pcworld.com/
Software Digest	http://www.nstl.com/swd.htm
Software Quarterly	http://pscc.dfw.ibm.com/sq/
Telecommunications Report	http://textor.iserver.com/cms/dBRTRE.html
Web Week	http://www.webweek.com/
WebMaster	http://www.cio.com/WebMaster
WebServer	http://www.cpg.com/ws/
Websight	http://websight.com/
Windows Magazine	http://www.winmag.com/
Windows Sources	http://www.zdnet.com/wsources/
Ziff-Davis Publishing	http://www5.zdnet.com/

APPENDIX C

This appendix gives job descriptions for computer-related careers. Read through them all for a general idea of what each position entails. If any sounds particularly interesting to you, do some research to decide if it's a profession you'd consider pursuing.

RELATED COMPUTER CAREERS

This appendix contains descriptions of jobs related to computer technician. You might consider entering the job market as a computer technician and then pursuing more training to work your way into one of these jobs.

Computer Operator

A computer operator generally works on the daily operations of a mainframe-type of computer. Their duties are to perform system backups, operate computer printers, run and distribute nightly reports, process scheduled jobs, and run file servers. A computer operator typically works on equipment such as AS400, UNIX, NT, and ES9000.

Database Administrator

A database administrator is responsible for the integrity of the databases on a network. In the case of a new database, the administrator helps define the data and tables and relationship between the pieces of data. As maintenance, the administrator creates and maintains indexing functions, and adds new tables to the database as required.

Network Administrator

A network administrator is responsible for creating, configuring, and maintaining a combination of servers and network technology. The configuration might exist on a Local Area Network (LAN) or a Wide Area Network (WAN). Server types include Novell, NT, and UNIX. Network technology includes TCPIP and NetBEUI.

Programmer

A computer programmer is an expert at one or more computer languages and scripts and uses them to create the applications that run on a computer. Examples of languages are C, C++, Java, Perl, Visual Basic, and MS Access.

Webmaster

A webmaster is the person responsible for posting files to the web server and configuring and maintaining the web server. Knowledge of servers, HTML, and Java is generally required.

Web Designer

A web designer is the person who, using HTML, JAVA, graphics, and a variety of software tools, actually creates the web pages. This position requires good writing and graphic skills, knowledge of online design, and some HTML/Java programming. A web designer can be responsible for:

- developing company Internet and intranet publications to meet the informational and promotional needs of the company
- developing ways for the company Internet sites to provide efficient and attractive means for potential customers to establish a useful connection to the company sales staff through coordination with marketing
- coordinating the informational and promotional needs of all departments to implement in the company web sites